Contents

How to use *Test it, Fix it*

Test it, Fix it is a series of books designed to help you identify any problems you may have in English, and to fix the problems. Each *Test it, Fix it* book has twenty tests which concentrate on mistakes commonly made by learners.

Test it, Fix it has an unusual format. You start at the **first** page of each unit, then go to the **third** page, then to the **second** page. Here's how it works:

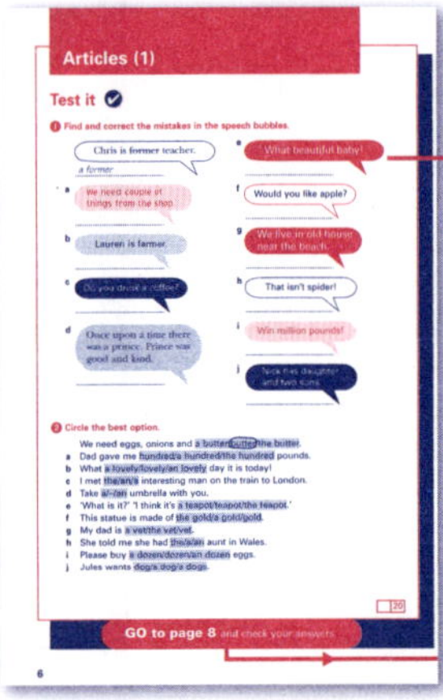
Articles (1)

Test it

1 Find and correct the mistakes in the speech bubbles.

Chris is former teacher. a former

a We need couple of things from the shop.

b Lauren is farmer.

c Do you drink a coffee?

d Once upon a time there was a prince. Prince was good and kind.

e What beautiful baby!

f Would you like apple?

g We live in old house near the beach.

h That isn't spider!

i Win million pounds!

j Nick has daughter and two sons.

2 Circle the best option.

We need eggs, onions and a butter/butter/the butter.

a Dad gave me hundred/a hundred/the hundred pounds.

b What a lovely/lovely/an lovely day it is today!

c I met the/an/a interesting man on the train to London.

d Take a/-/an umbrella with you.

e 'What is it?' 'I think it's a teapot/teapot/the teapot.'

f This statue is made of the gold/a gold/gold.

g My dad is a vet/the vet/vet.

h She told me she had the/a/an aunt in Wales.

i Please buy a dozen/dozen/an dozen eggs.

j Jules wants dog/a dog/a dogs.

20

GO to page 8 and check your answers

6

Test it (First page)

1. **Do the exercises on the *Test it* page.**

2. **Go to the *Fix it* page and check your answers before you do *Test it again*.**

Fix it (Third page)

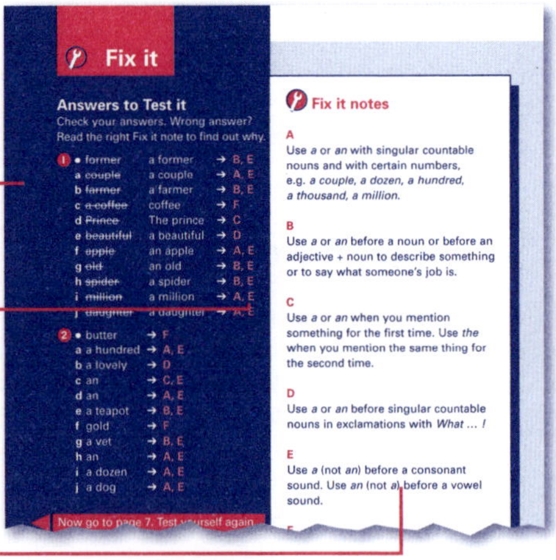
Fix it

Answers to Test it

Check your answers. Wrong answer? Read the right Fix it note to find out why.

1 • former a former → B, E
a couple a couple → A, E
b farmer a farmer → B, E
c a coffee coffee → F
d Prince The prince → C
e beautiful a beautiful → D
f apple an apple → A, E
g old an old → B, E
h spider a spider → B, E
i million a million → A, E
j daughter a daughter → A, E

2 • butter → F
a a hundred → A, E
b a lovely → D
c an → C, E
d an → A, E
e a teapot → B, E
f gold → F
g a vet → B, E
h an → A, E
i a dozen → A, E
j a dog → A, E

Now go to page 7. Test yourself again

Fix it notes

A
Use *a* or *an* with singular countable nouns and with certain numbers, e.g. *a couple, a dozen, a hundred, a thousand, a million.*

B
Use *a* or *an* before a noun or before an adjective + noun to describe something or to say what someone's job is.

C
Use *a* or *an* when you mention something for the first time. Use *the* when you mention the same thing for the second time.

D
Use *a* or *an* before singular countable nouns in exclamations with *What ... !*

E
Use *a* (not *an*) before a consonant sound. Use *an* (not *a*) before a vowel sound.

3. **Check your answers.**
   You can fold the page to make it easier to check.

4. **Wrong answer? Look for the *Fix it note* letter you need.**

5. **To understand why you made a mistake, read the *Fix it note*. If you need more information, read the *Review* page as well.**

6. **Now go back to the second page and do *Test it again*.**

Aurimas Grujauskas

Test it Fix it

Grammar

Intermediate

Kenna Bourke
with Peter May

OXFORD
UNIVERSITY PRESS

OXFORD
UNIVERSITY PRESS

Great Clarendon Street, Oxford OX2 6DP

Oxford University Press is a department of the University of Oxford.
It furthers the University's objective of excellence in research, scholarship, and education by publishing worldwide in

Oxford New York

Auckland Cape Town Dar es Salaam Hong Kong Karachi
Kuala Lumpur Madrid Melbourne Mexico City Nairobi
New Delhi Shanghai Taipei Toronto

With offices in

Argentina Austria Brazil Chile Czech Republic France Greece
Guatemala Hungary Italy Japan Poland Portugal Singapore
South Korea Switzerland Thailand Turkey Ukraine Vietnam

OXFORD and OXFORD ENGLISH are registered trade marks of Oxford University Press in the UK and in certain other countries

First published 2003
Revised version first published 2006
2010 2009 2008 2007 2006
10 9 8 7 6 5 4 3 2 1

ISBN-13: 978 0 19 439222 8
ISBN-10: 0 19 439222 8

Illustrated by Ken Pyne

Printed in Spain by Unigraf S.L.

Test it again (Second page)

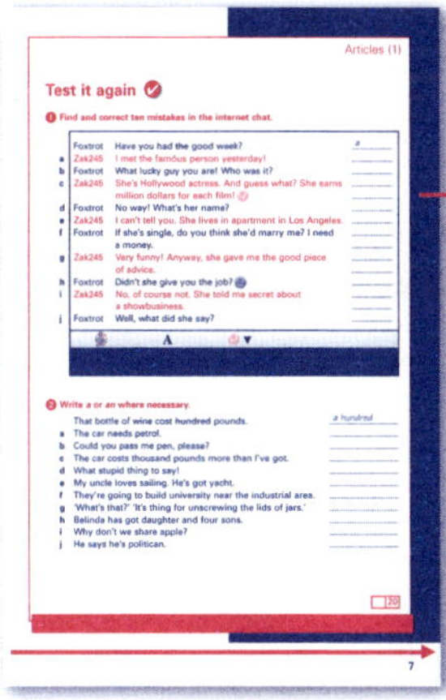
Articles (1)

Test it again

1 Find and correct ten mistakes in the internet chat.

	Foxtrot	Have you had the good week?	a
a	Zak245	I met the famous person yesterday!	
b	Foxtrot	What lucky guy you are! Who was it?	
c	Zak245	She's Hollywood actress. And guess what? She earns million dollars for each film!	
d	Foxtrot	No way! What's her name?	
e	Zak245	I can't tell you. She lives in apartment in Los Angeles.	
f	Foxtrot	If she's single, do you think she'd marry me? I need a money.	
g	Zak245	Very funny! Anyway, she gave me the good piece of advice.	
h	Foxtrot	Didn't she give you the job?	
i	Zak245	No, of course not. She told me secret about a showbusiness.	
j	Foxtrot	Well, what did she say?	

2 Write *a* or *an* where necessary.

	That bottle of wine cost hundred pounds.	a hundred
a	The car needs petrol.	
b	Could you pass me pen, please?	
c	The car costs thousand pounds more than I've got.	
d	What stupid thing to say!	
e	My uncle loves sailing. He's got yacht.	
f	They're going to build university near the industrial area.	
g	'What's that?' 'It's thing for unscrewing the lids of jars.'	
h	Belinda has got daughter and four sons.	
i	Why don't we share apple?	
j	He says he's politican.	

/20

7

7 Do the exercises on the *Test it again* page.

8 Go to the *Fix it* page and check your answers.

Fix it (Third page)

9 Check your answers.

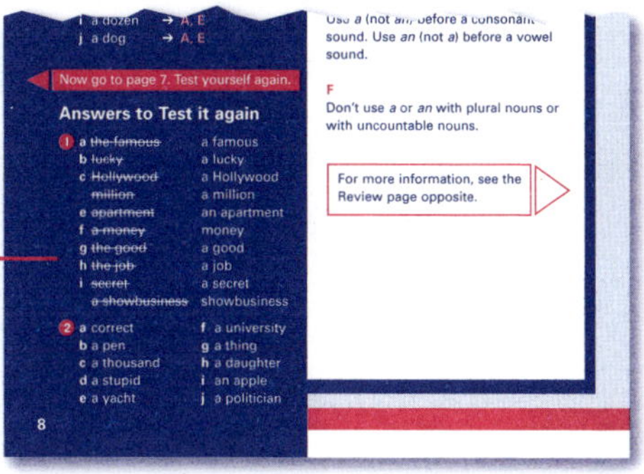
i a dozen → A, E
j a dog → A, E

Now go to page 7. Test yourself again.

Answers to Test it again

1 a ~~the famous~~ a famous
b ~~lucky~~ a lucky
c ~~Hollywood~~ a Hollywood
~~million~~ a million
e ~~apartment~~ an apartment
f ~~a money~~ money
g ~~the good~~ a good
h ~~the job~~ a job
i ~~secret~~ a secret
~~a showbusiness~~ showbusiness

2 a correct f a university
b a pen g a thing
c a thousand h a daughter
d a stupid i an apple
e a yacht j a politician

8

Use *a* (not *an*) before a consonant sound. Use *an* (not *a*) before a vowel sound.

F
Don't use *a* or *an* with plural nouns or with uncountable nouns.

For more information, see the Review page opposite.

Review (Fourth page)

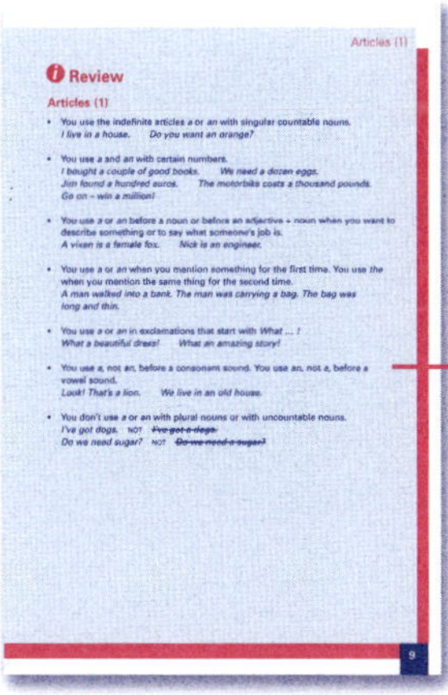
Articles (1)

Review

Articles (1)

- You use the indefinite articles *a* or *an* with singular countable nouns.
I live in a house. Do you want an orange?
- You use *a* and *an* with certain numbers.
I bought a couple of good books. We need a dozen eggs. Jim found a hundred euros. The motorbike costs a thousand pounds. Go on – win a million!
- You use *a* or *an* before a noun or before an adjective + noun when you want to describe something or to say what someone's job is.
A vixen is a female fox. Nick is an engineer.
- You use *a* or *an* when you mention something for the first time. You use *the* when you mention the same thing for the second time.
A man walked into a bank. The man was carrying a bag. The bag was long and thin.
- You use *a* or *an* in exclamations that start with *What ...!*
What a beautiful dress! What an amazing story!
- You use *a*, not *an*, before a consonant sound. You use *an*, not *a*, before a vowel sound.
Look! That's a lion. We live in an old house.
- You don't use *a* or *an* with plural nouns or with uncountable nouns.
I've got dogs. NOT ~~*I've got a dogs.*~~
Do we need sugar? NOT ~~*Do we need a sugar?*~~

9

10 You can read this page at any time. It gives you extended *Fix it* notes and example sentences. It's designed to give you a summary of the grammar you need for the whole test.

Articles (1)

Test it ✔

1 Find and correct the mistakes in the speech bubbles.

Chris is ~~former~~ teacher.
a former

a We need ~~couple~~ of things from the shop.

b Lauren is farmer.

c Do you drink a coffee?

d Once upon a time there was a prince. Prince was good and kind.

e What beautiful baby!

f Would you like apple?

g We live in old house near the beach.

h That isn't spider!

i Win million pounds!

j Nick has daughter and two sons.

2 Circle the best option.

We need eggs, onions and a butter/(butter)/the butter.

a Dad gave me hundred/a hundred/the hundred pounds.
b What a lovely/lovely/an lovely day it is today!
c I met the/an/a interesting man on the train to London.
d Take a/–/an umbrella with you.
e 'What is it?' 'I think it's a teapot/teapot/the teapot.'
f This statue is made of the gold/a gold/gold.
g My dad is a vet/the vet/vet.
h She told me she had the/a/an aunt in Wales.
i Please buy a dozen/dozen/an dozen eggs.
j Jules wants dog/a dog/a dogs.

/20

GO to page 8 and check your answers.

Test it again ✔

1 Find and correct ten mistakes in the internet chat.

	Foxtrot	Have you had ~~the~~ good week?	*a*
a	Zak245	Yes! I met the famous person yesterday!	
b	Foxtrot	What lucky guy you are! Who was it?	
c	Zak245	She's Hollywood actress. And guess what? She earns million dollars for each film! 😊	
d	Foxtrot	No way! What's her name?	
e	Zak245	I can't tell you. She lives in apartment in Los Angeles.	
f	Foxtrot	If she's single, do you think she'd marry me? I need a money.	
g	Zak245	Very funny! Anyway, she gave me the good piece of advice.	
h	Foxtrot	Didn't she give you the job? 😕	
i	Zak245	No, of course not. She told me secret about a showbusiness.	
j	Foxtrot	Well, what did she say?	

A ▼

Send

2 Write *a* or *an* where necessary.

	We need ~~hundred~~ coupons to get the palmtop.	*a hundred*
a	The car needs petrol.	
b	Could you pass me pen, please?	
c	The car costs thousand pounds more than I've got.	
d	What stupid thing to say!	
e	My uncle loves sailing. He's got yacht.	
f	They're going to build university near the industrial area.	
g	'What's that?' 'It's thing for unscrewing the lids of jars.'	
h	Belinda has got daughter and four sons.	
i	Why don't we share apple?	
j	He says he's politican.	

20

Fix it

Answers to Test it

Check your answers. Wrong answer? Read the right Fix it note to find out why.

1
- • ~~former~~ a former → B, E
- **a** ~~couple~~ a couple → A, E
- **b** ~~farmer~~ a farmer → B, E
- **c** ~~a coffee~~ coffee → F
- **d** ~~Prince~~ The prince → C
- **e** ~~beautiful~~ a beautiful → D
- **f** ~~apple~~ an apple → A, E
- **g** ~~old~~ an old → B, E
- **h** ~~spider~~ a spider → B, E
- **i** ~~million~~ a million → A, E
- **j** ~~daughter~~ a daughter → A, E

2
- • butter → F
- **a** a hundred → A, E
- **b** a lovely → D
- **c** an → C, E
- **d** an → A, E
- **e** a teapot → B, E
- **f** gold → F
- **g** a vet → B, E
- **h** an → A, E
- **i** a dozen → A, E
- **j** a dog → A, E

Now go to page 7. Test yourself again.

Answers to Test it again

1
- **a** ~~the famous~~ a famous
- **b** ~~lucky~~ a lucky
- **c** ~~Hollywood~~ a Hollywood
- ~~million~~ a million
- **e** ~~apartment~~ an apartment
- **f** ~~a money~~ money
- **g** ~~the good~~ a good
- **h** ~~the job~~ a job
- **i** ~~secret~~ a secret
- ~~a showbusiness~~ showbusiness

2
- **a** correct
- **b** a pen
- **c** a thousand
- **d** a stupid
- **e** a yacht
- **f** a university
- **g** a thing
- **h** a daughter
- **i** an apple
- **j** a politician

Fix it notes

A

Use *a* or *an* with singular countable nouns and with certain numbers, e.g. *a couple, a dozen, a hundred, a thousand, a million.*

B

Use *a* or *an* before a noun or before an adjective + noun to describe something or to say what someone's job is.

C

Use *a* or *an* when you mention something for the first time. Use *the* when you mention the same thing for the second time.

D

Use *a* or *an* before singular countable nouns in exclamations with *What … !*

E

Use *a* (not *an*) before a consonant sound. Use *an* (not *a*) before a vowel sound.

F

Don't use *a* or *an* with plural nouns or with uncountable nouns.

For more information, see the Review page opposite.

Review

Articles (1)

- You use the indefinite articles *a* or *an* with singular countable nouns.
  I live in a house.   *Do you want an orange?*

- You use *a* and *an* with certain numbers.
  I bought a couple of good books.   *We need a dozen eggs.*
  Jim found a hundred euros.   *The motorbike costs a thousand pounds.*
  Go on – win a million!

- You use *a* or *an* before a noun or before an adjective + noun when you want to describe something or to say what someone's job is.
  A vixen is a female fox.   *Nick is an engineer.*

- You use *a* or *an* when you mention something for the first time. You use *the* when you mention the same thing for the second time.
  A man walked into a bank. The man was carrying a bag. The bag was long and thin.

- You use *a* or *an* in exclamations that start with *What ... !*
  What a beautiful dress!   *What an amazing story!*

- You use *a*, not *an*, before a consonant sound. You use *an*, not *a*, before a vowel sound.
  Look! That's a lion.   *We live in an old house.*

- You don't use *a* or *an* with plural nouns or with uncountable nouns.
  I've got dogs. NOT ~~*I've got a dogs.*~~
  Do we need sugar? NOT ~~*Do we need a sugar?*~~

Articles (2)

Test it ✔

1 Tick the correct sentence in each pair.

	I'll meet you outside Colosseum.	☐
	I'll meet you outside the Colosseum.	☑
a	John, could you feed a cat, please?	☐
b	John, could you feed the cat, please?	☐
c	I really love the Mediterranean.	☐
d	I really love Mediterranean.	☐
e	Oonagh and I have same sense of humour.	☐
f	Oonagh and I have the same sense of humour.	☐
g	Shall we go by car or by train?	☐
h	Shall we go by the car or by the train?	☐
i	Have you seen the Lake Geneva?	☐
j	Have you seen Lake Geneva?	☐

2 Circle the best option, A or B.

Our house is second on ....
A right (**B**) the right

a Don't look at .... It's bad for your eyes.
A sun **B** the sun

b What would you like for .... tonight?
A the supper **B** supper

c They sent him to .... for ten years.
A prison **B** the prison

d Are you vegetarian or do you eat .... ?
A meat **B** the meat

e .... Malcolm Smith was a wonderful teacher.
A The professor **B** Professor

f He always goes to work ....
A on foot **B** on the foot

g Do we need to buy .... ?
A the salt **B** salt

h Sally's dream is to cross .... by camel.
A the Sahara **B** Sahara

i Paddy was born on .... 4 October.
A Tuesday **B** the Tuesday

j Have you seen .... ?
A Tower of London **B** the Tower of London

☐ 15

GO to page 12 and check your answers.

Test it again ✓

1 Find and correct the mistakes in these sentences.

Mack Snickler has been ~~in the prison~~ for sixteen years. .... *in prison*

- **a** Your briefcase is in kitchen, darling. Don't forget to take laptop. ....
- **b** When did Pope last visit France? Was it at the Christmas? ....
- **c** Freddy's at school. He'll be home later. He travels by the bus. ....
- **d** I'm so thirsty! I need water. But it has to be mineral water. ....
- **e** Do you celebrate Christmas? I love giving and receiving presents. ....
- **f** He doesn't believe that men have landed on moon. The surface of the planet is like Sahara Desert. ....
- **g** Jeff wants to climb Mount Everest. Then he wants to sail across Atlantic Ocean. ....
- **h** They're coming by train this time. They're spending Easter with us. ....
- **i** Have you had breakfast already? The others are still in bed. ....
- **j** The bank is on left, just past the post office but before you get to town hall. ....

2 Find and correct ten mistakes in these children's sentences.

I have cereal for ~~the breakfast~~.
breakfast

- **a** I love world because it's a beautiful place. ....
- **b** Stratford is on river Avon. Shakespeare lived there. ....
- **c** We're twins. We wear same clothes. ....
- **d** My favourite thing is travelling by the double-decker bus! ....
- **e** I hate the fish. I never eat it. ....
- **f** The best time of the year is the Christmas. ....
- **g** My rabbit's in garden. He's happy. ....
- **h** Mummy's at the work. ....
- **i** I like the Mrs Simmons. She's a nice teacher. ....
- **j** I'm sad because Daddy's in the hospital. ....

☐ 20

Fix it

Answers to Test it

Check your answers. Wrong answer? Read the right Fix it note to find out why.

1 The correct sentences are:

● → D	b → A	c → D
f → C	g → G	j → E

2

● B → C	a B → B	b B → E
c A → F	d A → H	e B → E
f A → G	g B → H	h A → D
i A → E	j B → D	

Now go to page 11. Test yourself again.

Answers to Test it again

1

a	~~in kitchen~~	in the kitchen
	~~take laptop~~	take the laptop
b	~~did Pope~~	did the Pope
	~~at the Christmas~~	at Christmas
c	~~by the bus~~	by bus
d	correct	
e	correct	
f	~~on moon~~	on the moon
	~~like Sahara Desert~~	like the Sahara Desert
g	~~across Atlantic Ocean~~	across the Atlantic Ocean
h	correct	
i	correct	
j	~~on left~~	on the left
	~~get to town hall~~	get to the town hall

2

a	~~world~~	the world
b	~~on river Avon~~	on the river Avon
c	~~same clothes~~	the same clothes
d	~~by the double-decker bus~~	by double-decker bus
e	~~the fish~~	fish
f	~~the Christmas~~	Christmas
g	~~in garden~~	in the garden
h	~~at the work~~	at work
i	~~the Mrs Simmons~~	Mrs Simmons
j	~~in the hospital~~	in hospital

Fix it notes

A

Use *the* when it's obvious which person or thing you're talking about.

B

Use *the* when the thing you're talking about is unique: there's only one.

C

Use *the* before some common expressions, e.g. *the same, the left*.

D

Use *the* with the names of places that are plural and with the names of deserts, seas, rivers, oceans and most buildings.

E

Don't use an article with meals, days, months, holidays, special days or festivals; or to talk about a person, a language or most places, including countries, mountains or lakes.

F

Don't use an article with some common expressions relating to places, e.g. *to prison, at school, in bed*.

G

Don't use an article with methods of transport, e.g. *by car, on foot*.

H

Don't use an article when you're talking about things in a general way.

For more information, see the Review page opposite.

Review

Articles (2)

- You use the definite article *the* when it's obvious which person or thing you're talking about.
  The rabbit's in the garden. (It's our rabbit and our garden.)
  Your glasses are on the table. (You know which table I mean.)

- You use *the* when the thing you're talking about is unique: there's only one.
  Don't stare at the sun. *Have you ever seen the Queen?*

- You use *the* before some common expressions.
  You and I both like the same things. *The office is on the right.*
  We love going to the theatre.

- You use *the* with the names of places that are plural. You also use *the* with the names of deserts, seas, rivers, oceans, and with the names of most buildings.
  Have you ever been to the Netherlands? *I spent some time in the Gobi Desert.*
  Rome is on the Tiber. *The ship sailed across the Pacific Ocean.*
  The Empire State Building is magnificent.

- You don't use an article with meals, days, months, holidays or festivals.
  Let's have dinner together. *My new job starts on Monday.*
  What are you doing at Easter?

- You don't use an article to talk about a person, a language or most places, including the name of a country, a mountain or a lake.
  Dr Sherringham is looking after me.
  NOT ~~*The Dr Sherringham is looking after me.*~~
  Maria's coming over later. NOT ~~*The Maria's coming over later.*~~
  I like Italian – it's a lovely language. *The children grew up in France.*
  Mont Blanc is a beautiful mountain. *Have you been to Lake Como?*

- You don't use an article with some common expressions, e.g. *in bed, in hospital, in prison; at home, at school, at work* or with methods of transport, e.g. *on foot, by bike, by train.*
  Jack's in prison again. NOT ~~*Jack's in the prison again.*~~
  Why is she in bed? *I'll be at home if you need me.*
  She prefers to travel by train. *It's not far – let's go by bike.*

- You don't use an article when you're talking about things in a general way.
  I love seafood. (seafood in general; all seafood)
  She doesn't eat meat. (any sort of meat; she's vegetarian)

Quantifiers

Test it ✓

1 Complete the sentences. Use *a*, *an*, *some* or *any*.

Would you like ..a....... cup of tea?

a Fred usually takes .... sandwiches and an orange to school.

b Did they give you .... information?

c No, sorry, I haven't got .... cigarettes. I don't smoke.

d Basil sent me .... postcard from Moscow.

e I'd like .... kilo of cherries, please.

f Nicola has had .... bad news.

g She says she can't give us .... advice. She's never been to Paris.

h Have .... more coffee. There's enough for both of us.

i Can you believe it? The supermarket didn't have .... meat!

j Pete's got .... money for you.

2 Circle the best option, A or B.

Zoe lent me .... money.
A any (**B**) some

a Patricia hasn't made .... new friends yet.
A any **B** some

b We can give you .... money if you need it.
A a few **B** a little

c She wants .... material to make a skirt.
A a **B** a metre of

d Do you own .... house or do you rent?
A any **B** a

e There are .... people still dancing.
A a few **B** many

f There isn't .... time before the show starts.
A much **B** a little

g Tom's got .... children to look after this weekend.
A many **B** a lot of

h The house really needs .... more pictures.
A a few **B** a little

i Could I have .... sugar in my coffee, please?
A a few **B** a little

j Let me give you .... advice.
A an **B** a piece of

[ ] 20

GO to page 16 and check your answers.

Test it again

1 Find and correct the mistakes in the sentences.

It was ~~some~~ very good piece of advice, to accept the job. ...a...

- **a** When we were in the forest, we saw many owls. In fact I've never seen so many in one place before. ....
- **b** I really don't want some information at all about interest rates. ....
- **c** Can you give Oscar a little biscuits? Just one or two. ....
- **d** I know you love this cheese. Would you like any more? ....
- **e** There aren't a few sunny days at this time of the year, so let's go to the beach today. ....
- **f** How much times have I told you not to do that? ....
- **g** Hurry up! We haven't got many time left. It starts in five minutes! ....
- **h** You've got many books, haven't you? ....
- **i** There isn't some butter, so please buy some. ....
- **j** Harry found some bone in the garden. It was horrible. ....

2 Complete the sentences. Use one word in each space.

bars *bottles* *can* *cartons* *cup* *~~kilo~~*
litres *metre* *piece* *slice* *tube*

It's outrageous! They're charging six euros for a ...kilo... of potatoes.

- **a** Let's take two .... of champagne to the party.
- **b** Oh yuck! I thought that was a .... of toothpaste, but it's shaving foam!
- **c** Would you like a .... of coffee?
- **d** Bill gave me an interesting .... of information today.
- **e** Go on, have another .... of cake. Forget the diet.
- **f** Could you buy me two .... of orange juice, please?
- **g** No wonder you've got toothache. You eat three .... of chocolate a day.
- **h** Everyone should drink two .... of water every day.
- **i** How much does a .... of this material cost?
- **j** Do you want a .... of Coke?

[ ] 20

Fix it

Answers to Test it

Check your answers. Wrong answer? Read the right Fix it note to find out why.

1
- • a → A, G
- **a** some → B
- **b** any → C
- **c** any → C
- **d** a → A
- **e** a → A, G
- **f** some → B
- **g** any → C
- **h** some → B
- **i** any → C
- **j** some → B

2
- • B → B
- **a** A → C
- **b** B → E
- **c** B → G
- **d** B → A
- **e** A → D
- **f** A → E
- **g** B → F
- **h** A → D
- **i** B → E
- **j** B → G

Now go to page 15. Test yourself again.

Answers to Test it again

1
- **a** ~~many~~ a lot of
- **b** ~~some~~ any
- **c** ~~a little~~ a few/some
- **d** ~~any~~ some
- **e** ~~a few~~ many
- **f** ~~much~~ many
- **g** ~~many~~ much
- **h** ~~many~~ a lot of
- **i** ~~some~~ any
- **j** ~~some~~ a

2
- **a** bottles
- **b** tube
- **c** cup
- **d** piece
- **e** slice
- **f** cartons
- **g** bars
- **h** litres
- **i** metre
- **j** can

Fix it notes

A

Use *a* or *an* with singular countable nouns.

B

Use *some* in positive sentences with plural countable nouns and uncountable nouns. Also use *some* in offers when you expect the answer to be 'Yes'.

C

Use *any* in negative sentences and in most questions with plural countable nouns and uncountable nouns.

D

Use *a few* in positive sentences with plural countable nouns.

E

Use *a little* in positive sentences with uncountable nouns. Use *not much* in negative sentences with uncountable nouns.

F

Use *a lot of* (not *many*) in positive sentences with plural countable nouns.

G

Use *a kilo*, *a litre*, *a metre*, etc. to talk about the quantity of uncountable nouns which you can measure. Use *a bottle*, *a tin*, *a box*, *a piece*, *a slice*, etc. to talk about the quantity of other uncountable nouns.

For more information, see the Review page opposite.

Review

Quantifiers

A, some and *any*

- You use the indefinite articles *a* or *an* with singular countable nouns.
  She'd like a job. *Please have an orange.*

- You use *some* in positive sentences with plural countable nouns and uncountable nouns. You also use *some* in offers when you expect the answer to be 'Yes'.
  He has some great ideas. *There's some good weather coming soon.*
  Do you want some more potatoes? *Would you like some more meat?*

- You use *any* in negative sentences and in most questions with plural countable nouns and uncountable nouns.
  There aren't any newspapers left in the shop. *Is there any water?*

A few, a little and *a lot of*

- You use *a few* in positive sentences with plural countable nouns. You use *not many*, or *how many* in negative sentences and questions with plural countable nouns.
  You can have a few more minutes to decide.
  There aren't many people here. *How many times have you met him?*

- You use *a little* in positive sentences with uncountable nouns and *not much* or *how much* in negative sentences and questions with uncountable nouns.
  He's saved a little money. *We haven't got much time.*
  How much information do you need?

- You use (*not*) *a lot of* in positive and negative sentences and in questions with plural countable nouns and with uncountable nouns.
  There's a lot of work to do. *Pat hasn't got a lot of friends.*
  Is there a lot of chicken left?

Measuring uncountable nouns

- You can make uncountable nouns countable in several ways.
  1. You can use expressions like *a kilo of, a litre of, a metre of*, etc.
     A kilo of carrots, please. *Add half a litre of milk.*
  2. You can describe the container that the noun is in, e.g. *a bag of, a can of*.
     We need a bag of flour. *I'll have a can of Coke.*
  3. You can divide the noun into separate parts, e.g. *a lump of, a piece of*.
     I'll have a slice of bread for lunch. *Mum gave me a good piece of advice.*

Possessive adjectives and pronouns

Test it ✔

1 Tick the correct sentence in each pair.

	Here's your cheque.	☑
	Here's you cheque.	☐
a	This is garden my.	☐
b	This is my garden.	☐
c	Adam's broken the arm.	☐
d	Adam's broken his arm.	☐
e	That money is to her!	☐
f	That money is hers!	☐
g	The cat has hurt its tail.	☐
h	The cat has hurt it's tail.	☐
i	That car is ours.	☐
j	Ours is that car.	☐

2 Complete the sentences. Use a possessive adjective or pronoun.

Don't forget to give the children *their* lunch.

a Hey! You can't take that, it's .... I bought it yesterday.

b Mike, this is Peter and this is .... girlfriend, Liz.

c Richard, are these keys .... ? They don't belong to me.

d Give that doll back to Jenny. It's ....

e Darling, what are we going to do? .... house is too small for us.

f Now that the dog has found .... ball, it's happy again.

g No, don't worry. I'll deal with it. After all, it's .... problem.

h Jo, don't blame me! The decision was ....

i They swapped .... car for a newer model and they love it.

j Anna's spilt coffee on .... shirt.

☐ 15

GO to page 20 and check your answers.

Test it again

1 Circle the best option.

Which of these coats is yours/your?
- **a** Lucy closed her/the eyes and fell asleep.
- **b** Tony is a good friend of me/mine.
- **c** No, that's not James and Kate's car. Their/Theirs is red.
- **d** Here's our/ours report. I hope you like it.
- **e** Look – that lorry's lost it's/its back wheel.
- **f** Danny, please take your hands out of the/your pockets.
- **g** You shouldn't take that. It's not yours/to you.
- **h** I'm sorry but I left mine/my homework on the bus.
- **i** Does this tractor belong to him/his?
- **j** Ouch! I've cut my/the finger!
- **k** Every time Sue and James come they leave their/theirs toothbrushes behind.
- **l** I'm sure that isn't to him/his – it looks just like the one I bought.
- **m** Its/It's a long time since we last met.
- **n** This horse can't jump very high because its/the legs are too short.

2 Choose the correct caption for the cartoon.

I've warned you before. It my bone is, not your, not his, MY!
I've warned you before. Its mine bone, not yours, not to him, MINE!
I've warned you before. It's my bone, not yours, not his, MINE!

[ ] 15

Fix it

Answers to Test it

Check your answers. Wrong answer?
Read the right Fix it note to find out why.

1 The correct sentences are:

- • → A
- b → C
- d → F
- f → B
- g → E
- i → D

2
- • their → A
- a mine → B
- b his/my → A
- c yours → B
- d hers → B
- e Our → A
- f its → A
- g my → A
- h yours → B
- i their → A
- j her → A

Now go to page 19. Test yourself again.

Answers to Test it again

1
- a her
- b mine
- c Theirs
- d our
- e its
- f your
- g yours
- h my
- i him
- j my
- k their
- l his
- m It's
- n its

2 I've warned you before. It's my bone – not yours, not his, MINE!

Fix it notes

A

Use a possessive adjective, e.g. *his*, *our*, to say who owns something or to talk about relationships between people.

B

Use a possessive pronoun, e.g. *hers*, *mine*, to replace a possessive adjective and a noun.

C

Always put the noun after (not before) the possessive adjective.

D

Always put the noun before (not after) the possessive pronoun.

E

Don't confuse the possessive adjective *its* with the contracted form *it's* (*it is*).

F

Use a possessive adjective (not *the*) to talk about clothes and parts of the body.

For more information, see the Review page opposite.

Review

Possessive adjectives and pronouns

- You use a possessive adjective (*my, your, his, her, its, our, their*) to say that something belongs to somebody or to talk about relationships between people.
  These are my DVDs. *Where are your brothers?*
  The goldfish just swims round its bowl all day long.

- You use a possessive pronoun (*mine, yours, his, hers, ours, theirs*) to replace a possessive adjective and a noun.
  These are my DVDs. ➔ *They're mine.* NOT ~~*They're to me.*~~
  ('Mine' replaces 'DVDs' and the possessive adjective.)
  That was his idea, not your idea. ➔ *It was his, not yours.*

- You always put the noun after (not before) the possessive adjective.
  Harry's my dog. NOT ~~*Harry's dog my.*~~
  There's your mother! NOT ~~*There's mother your!*~~

- You always put the noun before (not after) the possessive pronoun.
  This jacket's yours, isn't it? NOT ~~*This is yours jacket, isn't it?*~~
  The house is ours now! NOT ~~*Ours is the house now!*~~

- Try not to confuse the possessive adjective *its* with the contracted form *it's*, which means 'it is'.
  The fox takes good care of its cubs. NOT ~~*... it's cubs.*~~
  The computer's great. I love its keyboard. NOT ~~*...it's keyboard.*~~

  Note: Many native speakers of English make this mistake. You may see it on signs, on the internet and in some publications.

- You use a possessive adjective to talk about clothes and parts of the body. Don't use *the*.
  Pull your socks up. NOT ~~*Pull the socks up.*~~
  I banged my head. NOT ~~*I banged the head.*~~
  David's broken his leg. NOT ~~*David's broken the leg.*~~

Noun + noun

Test it ✓

1 Circle the best option, A, B or C.

2012 will be an American ....
A year election (**B**) election year **C** year of election

a Henry bought that book in a ....
A books shop **B** bookshop **C** book's shop

b We watched a great ....
A Japan film **B** Japan's film **C** film about Japan

c That's .... parked over there.
A my teacher's car **B** my teacher car **C** the car of my teacher

d I had to climb to .... to reach the cat.
A the ladder's top **B** the top of the ladder **C** the ladder top

e Freddy watched the ....
A match of football **B** football's match **C** football match

f Louise heard .... coming from the playroom.
A sounds of laughter **B** laughter's sounds **C** laughter sounds

g It's a .... flight to Seoul.
A twelve-hour **B** twelve hours' **C** twelve hours

h The Grand National is a famous .... It takes place once a year.
A racehorse **B** horse race **C** horses' race

i Do you like .... ?
A soup of tomato **B** tomatoes soup **C** tomato soup

j I prefer dark chocolate because .... is too sweet.
A milk's chocolate **B** chocolate milk **C** milk chocolate

2 True or false?

			True	False
	The edge of the cliff is ...	the cliff's edge.	☐	☑
a	The idea that Patrick had is ...	Patrick's idea.	☐	☐
b	The sink in the kitchen is ...	the kitchen's sink.	☐	☐
c	A book about cookery is ...	a cookbook.	☐	☐
d	A horse that you ride in races is ...	a horse race.	☐	☐
e	The nose that belongs to the dog is ...	the dog nose.	☐	☐
f	A card that shows your identity is ...	an identity card.	☐	☐
g	A thing you open a door with is ...	a door handle.	☐	☐
h	A book about maths is ...	a maths book.	☐	☐
i	A book about stars is ...	a stars book.	☐	☐
j	A shop that sells shoes is ...	a shoes shop.	☐	☐

☐ 20

GO to page 24 and check your answers.

Test it again ✓

1 What do you call …

a programme on TV? *a TV programme*

- **a** soup made of vegetables? ....
- **b** a shop where you buy stamps and post letters? ....
- **c** a boy who is ten years old? ....
- **d** a journey that is two hundred kilometres? ....
- **e** a brush that you brush your hair with? ....
- **f** a card that you send someone for a birthday? ....
- **g** food for cats? ....
- **h** a book that has 24 pages? ....
- **i** juice that is made from oranges? ....
- **j** an exercise on grammar? ....

2 Find and correct the mistake in each advert.

FOR SALE. ~~*DVD's player*~~. *£15 only!*
DVD player

a Eat corn's flakes for a good start to your day.
....

b The diet of Camilla is revolutionary. **Lose weight now!**
....

c Just opened – **new pet's shop.**
....

d **Computer's software at a discount. Hurry while stocks last.**
....

e Goldfish's bowl free. Mail me at jj@goldfish.net
....

f **Book of vocabulary just published.**
....

g Join our **ten kilometres** charity run!
....

h *Television's presenters needed.* Apply to Box 773.
....

i **Centre of leisure:** annual membership available.
....

j **Office of post for sale. £75,000 Tel: 08009 123 123**
....

[ ] 20

Fix it

Answers to Test it

Check your answers. Wrong answer? Read the right Fix it note to find out why.

1

- • B → A
- **a** B → A
- **b** C → B
- **c** A → C
- **d** B → B
- **e** C → A
- **f** A → B
- **g** A → A
- **h** B → A, D
- **i** C → A
- **j** C → A, D

2

- • False, the cliff edge → A
- **a** True → C
- **b** False, the kitchen sink → A
- **c** True → A
- **d** False, a racehorse → D
- **e** False, the dog's nose → C
- **f** True → A
- **g** True → A
- **h** True → A
- **i** False, a book about stars → B
- **j** False, a shoe shop → A

Now go to page 23. Test yourself again.

Answers to Test it again

1

- **a** vegetable soup
- **b** a post office
- **c** a ten-year-old boy
- **d** a two hundred-kilometre journey
- **e** a hairbrush
- **f** a birthday card
- **g** cat food
- **h** a 24-page book
- **i** orange juice
- **j** a grammar exercise

2

- **a** ~~corn's flakes~~ cornflakes
- **b** ~~The diet of Camilla~~ Camilla's diet
- **c** ~~pet's shop~~ pet shop
- **d** ~~Computer's~~ Computer
- **e** ~~Goldfish's~~ Goldfish
- **f** ~~Book of vocabulary~~ Vocabulary book
- **g** ~~ten kilometres~~ ten-kilometre
- **h** ~~Television's~~ Television
- **i** ~~Centre of leisure~~ Leisure centre
- **j** ~~Office of post~~ Post office

Fix it notes

A

Use noun + noun to talk about things that very often go together, e.g. *bookshop, football match, helicopter flight.*

B

Use a noun + preposition structure for things that don't go together very often, e.g. *a film about Japan, the top of the ladder, sounds of laughter.*

C

Use the possessive forms *'s* or *s'* to say that something belongs to someone.

D

The meaning changes if you reverse the word order.

For more information, see the Review page opposite.

Review

Noun + noun

- You use noun + noun to talk about things that very often go together, e.g. *bookshop, horse race, toothpaste, two-goal defeat*. Sometimes you write these as one word, sometimes as two or more words. If you're not sure, check in a dictionary. Often the first noun behaves like the object of a verb or preposition.
  Let's go to the bookshop. (The shop that sells books.)
  It was a great horse race. (A race between horses.)
  We need some more toothpaste. (The paste you use to clean your teeth.)

- You use a structure with a noun and a preposition (e.g. *for, from, about, of*) to talk about things that don't go together so often, e.g. *a book about animals, a film about China, the top of a hill.*
  Tom fell off the top of the ladder. NOT ~~the ladder's top~~
  NOT ~~the ladder top~~
  I saw a film about dolphins. NOT ~~a dolphin's film~~
  NOT ~~a dolphin film~~

- You use the possessive forms *'s* or *s'* to say that something belongs to someone. Often the first noun behaves like a subject.
  Don't pull the cat's tail! (The cat has a tail.) NOT ~~the cat tail~~
  NOT ~~the tail of the cat~~
  That's Dad's pen. (Dad has a pen.) NOT ~~Dad pen~~
  NOT ~~the pen of Dad~~

- With some noun + noun combinations, the meaning changes if you change the order of the two nouns.
  I need a phone card. (A card to make calls on a phone.)
  This is a card phone. (You can only use cards in this phone, not coins.)
  It's a horse race. (A race between horses.)
  It's a racehorse. (A horse that takes part in races.)

- Note that the form of one of the nouns may sometimes change.
  a car race (A race between cars.)
  a racing car (A car that takes part in races.)
  You need to check in a dictionary if you're not sure because you can't, for example, talk about ~~a racing horse~~.

Reflexive and emphatic pronouns

Test it ✔

1 Circle the best option.

Kate hurt her/(herself) when she fell off her bike.

- **a** We lost ourselves/got lost in the forest and couldn't find a way out.
- **b** The two men had an argument and then they started to hit each other/themselves.
- **c** Let's meet/meet ourselves after work for a drink.
- **d** I cut me/myself when I was chopping vegetables.
- **e** I got myself up/got up early this morning.
- **f** You stole it! You should be ashamed of/ashamed of yourself.
- **g** Haven't you got any money on you/yourself?
- **h** Eliza's only two and she can already dress herself/her.
- **i** We saved a lot of money by painting the house/by painting the house ourselves.
- **j** I'm glad Paula and John are getting married. They love themselves/each other very much.

2 Find and correct the mistakes in the sentences.

We gave ~~ourselves~~ the same present at Christmas. *each other*

- **a** Rachel was standing next to me. ....
- **b** After work, I like to relax myself at home. ....
- **c** It must be true. She told me her. ....
- **d** I'm not worried about Jane going alone. She can look after. ....
- **e** The Olympic champion himself will be swimming in the 200 metres. ....
- **f** Betty and her boyfriend decided to get engaged. ....
- **g** When the thief started to run away, the police officer shot himself. ....
- **h** Once they were friends, but now each other don't like. ....
- **i** Jamie burnt himself while he was cooking. ....
- **j** Who did your homework for you? No one. I did it myself. ....

☐ 20

GO to page 28 and check your answers.

Test it again ✓

1 Solve the clues to complete the crossword.

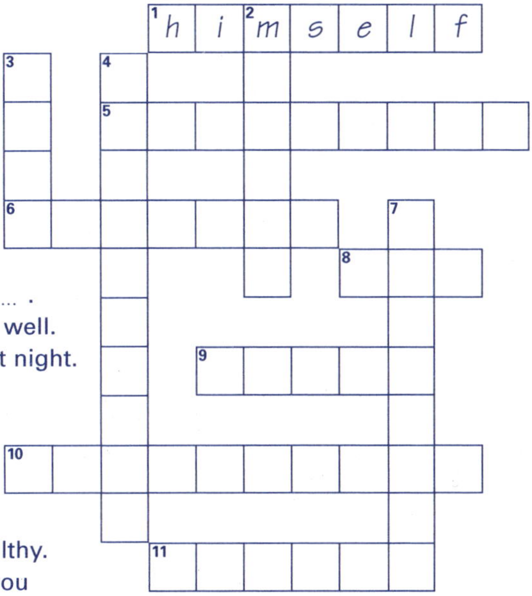

Across

1 John has bought .... a new house.

5 Why don't we repair the car .... ?

6 The Queen .... was at the show.

8 His parents .... divorced last year.

9 They congratulated each ....

10 The kids behaved .... very well.

11 The heating turns .... on at night.

Down

2 I enjoyed .... last night.

3 We see .... other every day.

4 Look at .... ! You're both filthy.

7 Ask .... this question: do you feel lucky?

2 Complete the sentences. Use reflexive pronouns or *each other*.

Einstein *himself* would have found the maths test hard.

a The two generals were enemies. They hated ....

b 'Did Ella have any help with the painting?' 'No, she did it ....'

c I made a terrible mistake. I was very angry with ....

d The girls were very vain. They looked at .... in the mirror all the time.

e One rider fell off his horse and injured ....

☐ 15

Fix it

Answers to Test it

Check your answers. Wrong answer?
Read the right Fix it note to find out why.

1
- • herself → A
- **a** got lost → F
- **b** each other → G
- **c** meet → C
- **d** myself → A
- **e** got up → C
- **f** ashamed of yourself → D
- **g** you → E
- **h** herself → A
- **i** by painting the house ourselves → B
- **j** each other → G

2

•	~~ourselves~~	each other	→ G
a	correct		→ E
b	~~relax myself~~	relax	→ C
c	~~her~~	herself	→ B
d	~~look after~~	look after herself	→ D
e	correct		→ B
f	correct		→ F
g	~~himself~~	him	→ A
h	~~each other don't like~~	they don't like each other	→ G
i	correct		→ A
j	correct		→ B

Now go to page 27. Test yourself again.

Answers to Test it again

1

			1 h	i	2 m	s	e	l	f	
3 e		4 y			y					
a		5 o	u	r	s	e	l	v	e	s
c		u			e					
6 h	e	r	s	e	l	f		7 y		
		s			f		8 g	o	t	
		e						u		
		l		9 o	t	h	e	r		
		v						s		
10 t	h	e	m	s	e	l	v	e	s	
		s						l		
			11 i	t	s	e	l	f		

2
- **a** each other
- **b** herself
- **c** myself
- **d** themselves
- **e** himself

Fix it notes

A
Use a reflexive pronoun if the subject and object of the verb are the same.

B
Use reflexive pronouns for emphasis: that person, nobody else. Or when someone does something without help.

C
Verbs that are reflexive in some languages may not be reflexive in English.

D
Use reflexive pronouns with some verbs + prepositions, e.g. *look at*, or phrasal verbs, e.g. *look after*, and after adjective + preposition, e.g. *ashamed of*.

E
Don't use reflexive pronouns after prepositions of place or position, e.g. *on*, *next to*.

F
Use *get* + past participle to make certain verbs reflexive, e.g. *get lost*, *get engaged*, *get divorced*.

G
Use *each other* (not *ourselves* or *themselves*) when two or more people do the same thing. Don't use *each other* as the subject of a verb.

For more information, see the Review page opposite.

Review

Reflexive and emphatic pronouns

Reflexive pronouns: *myself, yourself*, etc.

- You use a reflexive pronoun, e.g. *myself*, not a personal pronoun, e.g. *me*, when the subject and object of a verb are the same person or thing.
  I hurt myself in the accident. NOT ~~*I hurt me in the accident.*~~

- You can use reflexive pronouns to emphasize that someone or something can or can't do something without any help.
  Jo found herself a new boyfriend.
  He's broken his wrist, so he can't wash himself.

- You can also use reflexive pronouns to emphasize someone's importance.
  The Prime Minister himself was there.

- You can use reflexive pronouns with some verbs + prepositions, e.g. *believe in, look at*, with some phrasal verbs, e.g. *look after*, *take care of*, and with adjective + preposition, e.g. *ashamed of*. Don't use them after prepositions or expressions of place.
  You must believe in yourself. *Look at yourself. You're covered in mud!*
  My grandfather's ill because he doesn't take care of himself.
  NOT ~~*... take care of him.*~~
  I'm ashamed of myself for crying when I hurt my finger.
  There was a huge man in front of me. NOT ~~*... in front of myself.*~~

- Be careful! Some verbs are reflexive in some languages but not in English, e.g. *complain, concentrate, get up, go to bed, remember, rest, wonder.*
  I complained about the delay. NOT ~~*I complained myself about the delay.*~~

Get + past participle

- You can make some verbs reflexive by adding *get* to the past participle.
  I quickly got dressed. NOT ~~*I quickly dressed myself.*~~
  We got married last year. NOT ~~*We married ourselves last year.*~~
  They got up early. NOT ~~*They got up themselves early.*~~

Each other

- You use *each other* when two or more people do the same thing.
  We send each other birthday cards. (I send you a card and you send me a card.)
  Note that *We send ourselves birthday cards* means 'I send myself a card and you send yourself a card.'

- You use *each other* as the object of a verb, not as the subject of a verb.
  They understand each other. NOT ~~*Each other understands them.*~~

Adjectives and adverbs

Test it ✔

1 Tick the correct sentence in each pair.

	I felt badly about letting Jim down.	☐
	I felt bad about letting Jim down.	☑
a	These chocolates taste nice.	☐
b	These chocolates taste nicely.	☐
c	Frances wrote an excellent essay.	☐
d	Frances wrote a very excellent essay.	☐
e	Rabbits aren't aggressive animals.	☐
f	Rabbits aren't aggressives animals.	☐
g	There are some roads very narrow in Wales.	☐
h	There are some very narrow roads in Wales.	☐
i	Our little kitten ran around in a lively way.	☐
j	Our little kitten ran around livelily.	☐
k	My sister speaks fluently Italian.	☐
l	My sister speaks Italian fluently.	☐
m	The plane climbed high into the sky.	☐
n	The plane climbed highly into the sky.	☐
o	Karl plays the guitar brilliantly.	☐
p	Karl plays the guitar very brilliantly.	☐
q	Come into the house and get warmly.	☐
r	Come into the house and get warm.	☐
s	Jake's brother works very hard.	☐
t	Jake's brother works very hardly.	☐

2 Complete the sentences. Use the correct form of the words in brackets.

Mike seemed very *sad*.................................... (sad) yesterday.

a The children sang .... (loud) all the way home.

b Paul didn't look .... (comfortable) in those tight trousers.

c I must wake up .... (early) tomorrow morning.

d As a child, I often went to the park, but I haven't been there .... (late).

e Simon speaks German very .... (good).

☐ 15

GO to page 32 and check your answers.

Test it again ✔

1 Circle the best option, A or B.

The food in the canteen is ....
(**A**) terrible **B** very terrible

a I saw .... in the restaurant.
A an actor very famous **B** a very famous actor

b Jerry's voice sounded .... on the phone.
A strange **B** strangely

c You have to ....
A water often these plants **B** water these plants often

d New employees learn .... in this job.
A fast **B** fastly

e It is .... believed that Johnson is a criminal.
A wide **B** widely

f The fire .... destroyed the building.
A completely **B** very completely

g Our neighbour waved .... when he saw me.
A friendly **B** in a friendly way

h We drove .... because there was ice on the road.
A slow **B** slowly

i The government's economic policy is .... for the country.
A disastrous **B** very disastrous

j Open ....
A very carefully the packet **B** the packet very carefully

2 Find and correct the mistake in each advert.

Exclusive jewellery for ~~cheaps~~ prices!
cheap

a You don't have to work hardly to get rich.
....

b If your car always gets you to work lately, take a bus.
....

c To lose fast weight, join our fitness club.
....

d Wear the sunglasses that always look fashionably.
....

e You'll eat good at Ben's Burgers.
....

| /15

Fix it

Answers to Test it

Check your answers. Wrong answer? Read the right Fix it note to find out why.

1 The correct sentences are:

• → B	l → C
a → B	m → F
c → G	o → G
e → A	r → B
h → A	s → D, F
i → E	

2
- • sad → B
- a loudly → D
- b comfortable → B
- c early → D
- d lately → F
- e well → D

Now go to page 31. Test yourself again.

Answers to Test it again

1

a B	b A	c B	d A	e B
f A	g B	h B	i A	j B

2
- a ~~hardly~~ hard
- b ~~lately~~ late
- c ~~fast weight~~ weight fast
- d ~~fashionably~~ fashionable
- e ~~good~~ well

Fix it notes

A

Put adjectives before (not after) nouns or pronouns. Don't make adjectives plural.

B

Put adjectives (not adverbs) after these verbs: *appear, be, become, feel, get, look, seem, smell, sound, taste*.

C

Don't put adverbs between the verb and the object. Usually put them at the end of the sentence.

D

To form most adverbs, add *ly* to the adjective. Some adjectives and adverbs are irregular, e.g. *good/well*. Others, e.g. *early* and *hard*, have the same form for the adjective and the adverb.

E

Don't add *ly* to adjectives that already end in *ly*, e.g. *lively*. Use *in a ... way*.

F

Be careful! Some irregular adverbs that don't end in *ly*, e.g. *high* and *late*, also have *ly* forms but the meaning changes.

G

Don't use *very* with adjectives or adverbs like *excellent* or *brilliantly* which already mean 'very good', 'very well', etc.

For more information, see the Review page opposite.

Review

Adjectives and adverbs

- You put adjectives before (not after) nouns or pronouns.
  It's a beautiful song. NOT ~~*It's a song beautiful.*~~

- You can't make adjectives plural in English.
  He wears expensive clothes. NOT ~~*He wears expensives clothes.*~~

- You put adjectives (not adverbs) after (not before) these verbs: *appear, be, become, feel, get, look, seem, smell, sound, taste.*
  The flowers smell fresh. NOT ~~*The flowers fresh smell.*~~
  That food tasted horrible. NOT ~~*That food tasted horribly.*~~

- You make most adverbs by adding *ly* to the adjective, but some are irregular, e.g. *good/well.* You can often put adverbs at the end of a sentence, but not between a verb and its object.
  Henry solved the problem easily. NOT ~~*Henry solved easily the problem.*~~
  Lisa plays the saxophone well. NOT ~~*Lisa plays well the saxophone.*~~

- *Early, late, fast, hard, daily, weekly* and *monthly* can be adjectives and adverbs.
  She loves fast motorbikes. *Some people always walk fast.*

- You don't add *ly* to make adverbs from adjectives that already end in *ly*, e.g. *cowardly, friendly, kindly, lively, lonely.* For these words, you use a phrase with *way* or *manner.*
  They talked to me in friendly way. NOT ~~*They talked to me friendlily.*~~

- Some adverbs have two forms. The meaning changes.
  He always gets here late. (not at the right time)
  Have you seen her lately? (recently)
  I'll have to work hard. (I'll have to do a lot of work.)
  I can hardly see. (It's very difficult to see.)
  A bird flew high above. (up in the air)
  I think highly of you. (I admire you.)
  The window was wide open. (completely)
  It's widely known that he's dishonest. (Lots of people know this.)

- You can use *very* to make the meaning of many adjectives and adverbs stronger. However, you can't do this with adjectives and adverbs that already have strong meanings, e.g. *awful/awfully, brilliant/brilliantly, complete/completely, excellent/excellently, perfect/perfectly, terrible/terribly, wonderful/wonderfully.*
  Our holiday was awful. NOT ~~*Our holiday was very awful.*~~
  David, I think you're brilliant! NOT ~~*very brilliant*~~

Prepositions of place

Test it ✓

1 Circle the best option.

Ken and Kate first met at/(in)/by Rome.

a We waited at/in/on the bus stop.
b Toby is sitting at/among/between Ed and Sean.
c Is there a bank anywhere near/next to/beside here?
d I slept with just one sheet above/over/between me.
e Canada is next to/near/over the USA. You can cross the border from one country to the other.
f Have you spilt something in/on/at the carpet?
g I found a ring among/between/by the shells on the beach.
h There's a mobile phone mast on/over/between the roof.
i The hillstation of Nai Nital is at/in/on India.
j The garden is below/under/underneath the house. You go down some steps to get to it.

2 Complete the sentences. Use one word in each space.

in *on* *at* *among* *between* ~~*by*~~
near *above* *over* *under* *below*

Tom lives in a house ...*by*... the river.

a Jane bought a bottle of perfume .... the plane from Singapore.
b The village is 936 metres .... sea level, so it's cooler than it is on the coast.
c I'm sure there's a petrol station .... here. It can't be far away.
d Support for the president has fallen .... 50% for the first time since 2001.
e I enjoy spending the evening .... the cinema with my friends.
f The cat was stuck .... two chimneys. Firemen had to rescue it.
g The Sahara Desert is .... North Africa.
h The baby looks cold. Put another blanket .... him.
i If you cut your finger, put it .... the tap to wash it.
j He couldn't see me .... the crowds of people.

[ ] 20

GO to page 36 and check your answers.

Test it again ✓

1 Find and correct the mistakes in the sentences.

There's a new supermarket ~~next~~ the town hall. *next to*
- **a** That house is noisy because it's among four main roads. ....
- **b** If you need to get into the flat, there's a key below the mat. ....
- **c** Can you hear me? I'm on the train. ....
- **d** Jo sat down near to Ed and whispered something in his ear. ....
- **e** My grandfather always carried his coat over his arm. ....
- **f** There are some more clean towels in the second drawer. ....
- **g** The criminal had a blanket above his head to hide his face. ....
- **h** There must be a few good ones among all those CDs. ....
- **i** My sister's spending part of the summer holidays at China. ....
- **j** The climber is only 400 metres under the summit of Everest. ....
- **k** Una loved Jack and Simon. She couldn't choose between them. ....
- **l** The man had nowhere to go so he spent the night on his car. ....

2 Use a suitable preposition to complete the sentences. Sometimes there is more than one correct answer.

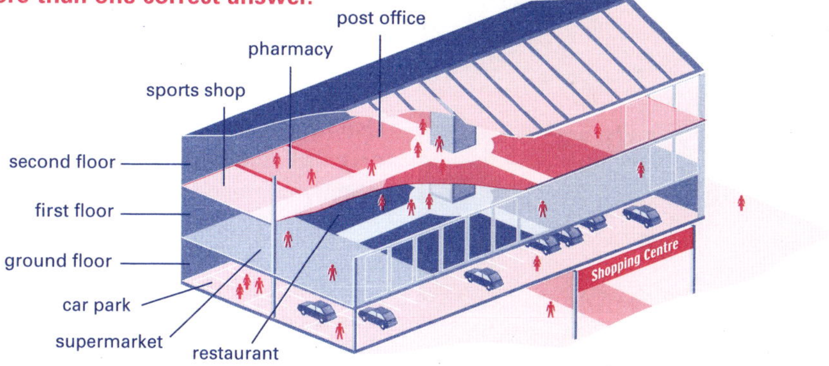

The supermarket is *under/below* the sports shop.
- **a** The supermarket is .... the shopping centre.
- **b** The sports shop is .... to the pharmacy.
- **c** The restaurant is .... the first floor.
- **d** The pharmacy is .... the sports shop and the post office.
- **e** The car park is .... the restaurant and the supermarket.
- **f** The post office is .... the restaurant.

☐ 18

Fix it

Answers to Test it

Check your answers. Wrong answer? Read the right Fix it note to find out why.

1
- • in → A
- **a** at → C
- **b** between → D
- **c** near → E
- **d** over → F
- **e** next to → E
- **f** on → B
- **g** among → D
- **h** on → B
- **i** in → A
- **j** below → G

2
- • by → E
- **a** on → B
- **b** above → F
- **c** near → E
- **d** below → G
- **e** at → C
- **f** between → D
- **g** in → A
- **h** over → F
- **i** under → G
- **j** among → D

Now go to page 35. Test yourself again.

Answers to Test it again

1
- **a** ~~among~~ between
- **b** ~~below~~ under/underneath
- **c** correct
- **d** ~~near to~~ next to/by/beside
- **e** correct
- **f** correct
- **g** ~~above~~ over
- **h** correct
- **i** ~~at~~ in
- **j** ~~under~~ below
- **k** correct
- **l** ~~on~~ in

2
- **a** in
- **b** next
- **c** on
- **d** between
- **e** under/below
- **f** above/over

Fix it notes

A

Use *in* for three-dimensional spaces, e.g. drawers, rooms, cities or countries.

B

Use *on* for two-dimensional surfaces, e.g. walls and floors, and for methods of transport, e.g. planes and buses (but not cars).

C

Use *at* for general points or positions and for buildings with people inside them.

D

Use *between* with people or things that are separate. Use *among* with people or things that are part of a group.

E

Use *near* when you mean 'not far away' or 'close' and *next to*, *by* or *beside* when you mean 'side by side'.

F

Use *over* when one thing covers, crosses or touches another thing. Use *above* when one thing is higher than another thing but not directly over it.

G

Use *under* if one thing covers, hides or touches another thing. Use *below* if one thing is at a lower level than another but not directly under it. Also use *below* with measurements.

For more information, see the Review page opposite.

Review

Prepositions of place

In, on, at

- You use *in* for three-dimensional spaces like boxes, rooms, cities and countries.
  There's some lovely furniture in this room. *The station is in the city centre.*

- You use *on* for two-dimensional surfaces like the pages of a book, screens or tables. You also use *on* for the position of something on a line, e.g. a road, and for methods of transport like bikes, buses and planes (but not cars).
  Rome is on the river Tiber. *It's on page two.* *Jim's on the bus.*

- You use *at* for general points, and for buildings when you're thinking about what people do inside them.
  Julia waited for an hour at the bus stop. *I worked hard at school today.*

Among, between

- You use *between* when you're talking about two or more people or things that are clearly separate. You use *among* when you're talking about a number of people or things that you don't see separately but as a group.
  The child stood between her parents. *They're between France and Spain.*
  Bob was somewhere among the crowd of 100,000.

Near, next to, by, beside

- You use *near* when people or things are in the same general area. You use *next to* for people or things that are side by side. You can also use *by* or *beside* to mean 'at the side of'.
  He lives near the old theatre. (His house is not far from the theatre.)
  The dictionary is next to the atlas. (There are no other books between them.)
  They have a beautiful house by the sea. *Come and sit beside me.*

Above, over; under, below

- *Above* and *over* can both mean 'higher than'. You use *above* when one thing is higher than another thing but not directly over it. You use *over* when one thing covers, crosses or touches another thing.
  There's a hot air balloon above/over that house.
  Please don't lean over my shoulder when I'm reading.

- *Under* and *below* can both mean 'lower than'. You use *below* when one thing is at a lower level than another but not directly under it. You also use *below* to talk about measurements, especially height, temperature or percentages. You use *under* when one thing covers, touches or hides another thing.
  The cupboard under/below the stairs is a mess. *Inflation is below 5%.*
  He's just below the summit of Everest. *It's hiding under the chair.*

Prepositions and expressions of time

Test it ✔

1 Find and correct five mistakes in the sentences.

	I'm going to London ~~on~~ the weekend.	at
a	I hate getting up on Monday morning!	....
b	Come and stay with us on July.	....
c	Please turn mobile phones off during the performance.	....
d	I'll be ready in a few minutes.	....
e	The show always starts in time, so don't be late.	....
f	Why do we go to the same place on every day?	....
g	We will now show this programme in 11.30.	....
h	If there are no delays, we'll be there by six.	....
i	She always wears that hat while the winter.	....
j	I'll wait here until the others arrive.	....

2 Circle the best option, A or B.

Daisy was born .... 12 August.
(**A**) on **B** at

a I'm meeting Danny .... half-past nine.
A on **B** at

b Stay here .... I go back for my books.
A during **B** while

c We'll wait .... ten, but then we'll have to go.
A until **B** by

d He'll be very tired .... the exams are over.
A by **B** by the time

e The carnival is .... the third week of April.
A in **B** at

f Were you at the concert .... Saturday?
A last **B** on last

g All the shops are busy .... New Year's Day.
A at **B** on

h We must receive your application .... 31 May.
A by **B** until

i We'll phone you back .... ten minutes.
A on **B** in

j We only got there .... for the flight because it was delayed.
A in time **B** on time

[   ] 20

GO to page 40 and check your answers.

Test it again

1 Circle the best option.

Spain is wonderful at/in/on the summer, and there's a lot for visitors to Madrid to do and see [a] at/in/on the weekend. [b] At/In/On Saturday there's a performance of Mozart's *Don Giovanni* at the National Auditorium, and in Retiro Park there's an open-air concert of South American folk music. That will go on [c] during/by/until about 2 a.m. For art lovers there's a special exhibition of Goya portraits at the Prado Gallery. This opens [d] at/in/on 9.30, but will be closed [e] during/while/by the time the afternoon from 2 to 5. It's also the last day of the Tour of Spain: [f] by/until/during the middle of the day, the leading cyclists will be racing through the city. As the main north-south road will be closed, don't expect the buses to run [g] at time/in time/on time! [h] On/–/In last year, they were running three hours late!

2 Complete the sentences. Use a preposition or a time expression where necessary.

Remember to post your letter *by*.................................... 5.00 p.m.

- **a** I listen to music .... I'm studying. It helps me concentrate.
- **b** If the train doesn't arrive .... , you get your money back.
- **c** I'll meet you .... tomorrow evening outside the cinema.
- **d** It's important that you start .... exactly 9.15.
- **e** We'll continue looking for the ship's crew .... we find them.
- **f** I asked them again .... last Wednesday.
- **g** The firm hope to complete the project .... less than a year.
- **h** I'm going to a meeting .... Friday, so I can't see you then.
- **i** Hurry up, or the shop will be shut .... we get there.
- **j** Belinda's husband didn't get to the hospital .... to see the baby being born.

/18

Fix it

Answers to Test it

Check your answers. Wrong answer? Read the right Fix it note to find out why.

1

•	~~on~~	at	→ A
a	correct		→ B
b	~~on~~	in	→ C
c	correct		→ E
d	correct		→ H
e	~~in~~	on	→ G
f	~~on~~	no preposition	→ D
g	~~in~~	at	→ A
h	correct		→ F
i	~~while~~	in	→ C
j	correct		→ F

2

• A → B
a B → A
b B → E
c A → F
d B → F
e A → C
f A → D
g B → B
h A → F
i B → H
j A → G

Now go to page 39. Test yourself again.

Answers to Test it again

1
a at
b On
c until
d at
e during
f by
g on time
h –

2
a while
b on time
c –
d at
e until
f –
g in
h on
i by the time
j in time

Fix it notes

A
Use *at* for times of the day and with words like *Christmas, the weekend,* etc.

B
Use *on* with days of the week and with dates, e.g. *Monday morning, New Year's Day.*

C
Use *in* with months, years, seasons, centuries, and with *the morning, the third week of April,* etc.

D
Don't use a preposition with *every day, last Saturday,* etc.

E
Use *during* with a noun. Use *while* with subject + verb.

F
Use *until* for 'up to a particular time or event' and *by* for 'not after a particular time or event'. Use *by the time* with subject + verb.

G
Use *on time* when you mean 'at exactly the right time' and *in time* when you mean 'early enough'.

H
Use *in* for the length of time something takes, e.g. *in a few minutes.*

For more information, see the Review page opposite.

Review

Prepositions and expressions of time

At, in, on

- You use *at* for clock time, times of the day, e.g. *lunchtime*, and in the expression *at night*. You also use *at* to talk about whole weekends and festivals.
  Let's meet at 5.30. *Where are you going at the weekend?*

- You use *on* with days of the week, dates, particular days during festivals and with expressions like *on Monday morning*.
  The exam is on Tuesday. *He was born on the fourth of July.*
  She goes swimming on Saturday mornings.

- You use *in* with months, years, seasons, centuries and with expressions like *in the first week of May* and *in the morning*.
  My birthday's in June. *That film came out in 2002.*
  Pop music began in the twentieth century. *I'd prefer to go in the afternoon.*

- You use *in* to talk about how long it takes to do something or to say how long it will be before something happens.
  He made his bed in 30 seconds. (It took him 30 seconds to make his bed.)
  I'll be at your place in ten minutes. (The journey will take ten minutes.)

- You don't use a preposition with expressions like *this week, every night*, etc.
  I see her every day. *I was out last night.* NOT ~~*I was out on last night.*~~

While, during, until, by

- You use *while* with a subject and verb, but *during* with a noun.
  I met him while I was on holiday. *I met him during the holidays.*

- You use *until* to say that something will continue to a particular time. To say 'not later than' you can use *by*.
  I'll stay until about 11.30. *You'll have to finish the job by Friday.*

In time, on time, by the time

- You use *on time* to say 'at exactly the right time', but *in time* to say 'not late'.
  The 6.30 train left on time. (It left on schedule at 6.30.)
  We got to the station in time. (We didn't miss the train.)

- You can use *by the time* before a subject and verb to mean 'not later than a particular event'.
  You'll have to finish the job by the time Sarah gets back.

Direct and indirect objects

Test it ✓

1 Tick the correct sentence in each pair.

Tim lent me his iPod. ☑
Tim lent to me his iPod. ☐

a I gave some flowers my mother. ☐
b I gave some flowers to my mother. ☐

c The teacher suggested a good dictionary to us. ☐
d The teacher suggested us a good dictionary. ☐

e John bought a necklace his wife. ☐
f John bought his wife a necklace. ☐

g Can you explain the word to me? ☐
h Can you explain me the word? ☐

i Give it to Billy. ☐
j Give Billy it. ☐

2 Find and correct the mistakes in the sentences.

I'll try to find ~~them you~~.
them for you

a Jake described us his house.
....

b Why don't you lend Kathy the car?
....

c Please read me a story.
....

d Show to me that photo.
....

e Luke suggested a brilliant restaurant to us.
....

f You owe me it!
....

g I want to some coffee make you.
....

h Can you buy me a paper?
....

i He wants to say 'Hello' to you.
....

j Johnny sang to us a song.
....

☐ 15

GO to page 44 and check your answers.

Test it again ✓

1 Write sentences.

explained / us / the problem / they / to
They explained the problem to us.

a to / my teacher / showed / it / I
....

b they / us / the news / gave
....

c get / a card / him / for / Vicky / will
....

d did / my book / you / her / lend
....

e me / Nick / didn't / an email / send
....

f have found / we / a hotel / you / for
....

g to / lend / him / it
....

h didn't / give / the job / Pete / to / they
....

2 Match a–k to 1–11.

a Steve wants	**1** goodbye to us.	**a** *11*
b Please give it	**2** said to him?	**b** ....
c Let's take Tony	**3** the bill?	**c** ....
d The dog bit	**4** her a happy New Year.	**d** ....
e He said	**5** the pyramids to me?	**e** ....
f Harry bought	**6** to Richard.	**f** ....
g Do you know what she	**7** the window cleaner.	**g** ....
h When will Dad teach	**8** to the beach.	**h** ....
i Could you send us	**9** me to drive?	**i** ....
j He wished	**10** Sally some chocolates.	**j** ....
k Can you describe	**11** to see you.	**k** ....

[ ] 18

Fix it

Answers to Test it

Check your answers. Wrong answer? Read the right Fix it note to find out why.

1 The correct sentences are:

- • → A
- b → B
- c → D, B
- f → A
- g → D, B
- i → C

2
- • ~~them you~~ them for you → C
- a us ~~his house.~~ his house to us. → D, B
- b correct → A
- c correct → A
- d ~~to me that photo.~~ that photo to me. → A, B
- e correct → D, B
- f ~~me it!~~ it to me! → C
- g ~~some coffee make you.~~ make you some coffee. → A
- h correct → A
- i correct → D, B
- j ~~to us a song.~~ a song to us. → A, B

Now go to page 43. Test yourself again.

Answers to Test it again

1
- a I showed it to my teacher.
- b They gave us the news.
- c Vicky will get a card for him.
- d Did you lend her my book?
- e Nick didn't send me an email.
- f We have found a hotel for you.
- g Lend it to him.
- h They didn't give the job to Pete.

2
a 11 b 6 c 8 d 7
e 1 f 10 g 2 h 9
i 3 j 4 k 5

Fix it notes

A

If the indirect object comes before the direct object, don't use *to* or *for*. But usually put the indirect object before (not after) the direct object.

B

When the indirect object comes after the direct object, use *to* or *for*.

C

When the direct object is a pronoun, e.g. *me*, *it*, *them*, put it before (not after) the indirect object and use *to* or *for*.

D

Put the indirect object after the direct object with the verbs *describe*, *explain*, *say* and *suggest*.

For more information, see the Review page opposite.

Review

Direct and indirect objects

It's usually easy to recognize a direct object in a simple sentence. For example, in the sentence 'Katy teaches maths', *maths* is the direct object. However, many verbs can have two objects – a direct object and an indirect object. Very often the indirect object is a person, and very often it goes before the direct object, like this: 'Katy teaches the children maths.' In this sentence *the children* is the indirect object.

- You usually put the indirect object before (not after) the direct object.
  Nicholas gave Gillian some flowers.
  (*Gillian* is the indirect object; *some flowers* is the direct object.)

- If you want to put the indirect object after the direct object, you use *to* or *for*.
  Nicholas gave some flowers to Gillian.
  Charlie made a card for his mother.

- You need to learn which verbs take *to*, and which take *for*. Here are the most common ones.
  Verb + *to*: *describe, explain, give, lend, say, send, show, suggest*
  Verb + *for*: *buy, find, get, make*

- When the direct object is a pronoun, e.g. *me, it, them*, you put it before (not after) the indirect object and you use *to* or *for*.
  Could you explain it to Lynn? *Please lend them to Teresa.*

- You put the indirect object after the direct object with the verbs *describe, explain, say* and *suggest*.

We described the house to our friends.	NOT	~~*We described our friends …*~~
I've come to say 'Hello' to you.	NOT	~~*… to say you 'Hello'.*~~
He suggested a great restaurant to us.	NOT	~~*He suggested us …*~~

Word order with verb + object

Test it ✓

1 Read the sentences. Are the statements about them true or false?

A Every Sunday, Hugo plays football.
B Hugo plays football every Sunday.
Both of these sentences are possible. True ☑ False ☐

a **A** He likes very much Italy.
B He likes Italy very much.
Both of these sentences are possible. True ☐ False ☐

b **A** We've lived here since 2001.
B We've since 2001 lived here.
Neither of these sentences is possible. True ☐ False ☐

c **A** Nick took Sally back home.
B Nick took back home Sally.
Only one of these sentences is possible. True ☐ False ☐

d **A** Jeff near Oxford lives.
B Jeff lives near Oxford.
Both of these sentences are possible. True ☐ False ☐

e **A** She loves you very much.
B She very much loves you.
Both of these sentences are possible. True ☐ False ☐

f **A** She went to the theatre last week.
B Last week she went to the theatre.
Both of these sentences are possible. True ☐ False ☐

g **A** Don't stay out too late.
B Don't too late stay out.
Neither of these sentences is possible. True ☐ False ☐

2 Find and correct the mistake in each sentence.

There's a festival ~~in the summer in Salzburg~~. *in Salzburg in the summer*

a I bought yesterday a jacket. ....

b He always gets early to the office. ....

c I lost my passport and I lost also my credit cards. ....

d David is Spanish but he speaks fluently English. ....

e Go past the bank and you'll see on the right the post office.

....

☐ 12

GO to page 48 and check your answers.

Test it again ✓

1 Find and correct the mistakes in the magazine headlines.

~~In local village~~ Football star buys mansion in local village.

a Fresh fruit and vegetables are good for you. Eat every day five portions.

b TV comic takes on holiday famous model – *but who is she?*

c Rock legend invites to his wedding five hundred guests!

d City council builds opposite the school a new leisure centre.

e Boy, 8, finds in the garden a tarantula.

2 Tick the best sentence in each pair.

Stan makes in his spare time model aeroplanes. ☐
Stan makes model aeroplanes in his spare time. ✓

a My dog doesn't like very much chocolate. ☐
b My dog doesn't like chocolate very much. ☐

c Every morning, we go swimming. ☐
d We go every morning swimming. ☐

e We dropped at the station Tony and Sally. ☐
f We dropped Tony and Sally at the station. ☐

g You shouldn't stay so long in bed. ☐
h You shouldn't stay in bed so long. ☐

i He wants a moped and he wants also a car. ☐
j He wants a moped and he also wants a car. ☐

☐ 10

Fix it

Answers to Test it

Check your answers. Wrong answer? Read the right Fix it note to find out why.

1
- • True, A and B are possible → E
- **a** False, only B is possible → A
- **b** False, A is possible → D
- **c** True, only A is possible → C
- **d** False, only B is possible → B
- **e** False, only A is possible → A
- **f** True, A and B are possible → E
- **g** False, A is possible → D

2
- • in Salzburg in the summer → D
- **a** I bought a jacket yesterday. → A
- **b** He always gets to the office early. → B, D
- **c** and I also lost my credit cards. → A
- **d** but he speaks English fluently. → A
- **e** you'll see the post office on the right. → C

Now go to page 47. Test yourself again.

Answers to Test it again

1
- **a** ~~every day five portions.~~ five portions every day.
- **b** ~~takes on holiday famous model~~ takes famous model on holiday
- **c** ~~to his wedding five hundred guests!~~ five hundred guests to his wedding!
- **d** ~~opposite the school a new leisure centre.~~ a new leisure centre opposite the school.
- **e** ~~in the garden a tarantula.~~ a tarantula in the garden.

2 The best sentences are:

b c f h j

Fix it notes

A

Put verbs and their objects together. Don't put other words between them.

B

Verbs and places usually go together, e.g. *live near Oxford, get to the office, stay in bed.*

C

If the verb has an object, put the place after (not before) the verb + object.

D

Usually put time expressions, e.g. *since 2001, every six months, in the winter, late, early,* after (not before) place.

E

Time expressions, e.g. *next Saturday, last week, every morning,* can sometimes go at the beginning or at the end of a sentence.

For more information, see the Review page opposite.

i Review

Word order with verb + object

- You put verbs and their objects together. You don't put other words between them. This is a very common mistake.
  I like Siena very much. NOT ~~*I like very much Siena.*~~
  He lost his passport. He also lost his wallet. NOT ~~*He lost also his wallet.*~~

- Verbs and places usually go together, e.g. *go to school, stay at home, walk to work*. You don't put other words between them.
  You shouldn't stay at home so much. NOT ~~*... so much at home.*~~
  He walks to work every day. NOT ~~*... every day to work.*~~

- If the verb has an object, you put the place after (not before) the verb + object.
  David took Maria home. NOT ~~*David took home Maria.*~~
  We met William in the supermarket. NOT ~~*... met in the supermarket William.*~~

- You usually put time expressions, e.g. *every day, next month, on Monday,* after (not before) place.
  I'm going to Korea next month. NOT ~~*... next month to Korea.*~~
  We go back to school on Monday. NOT ~~*...back on Monday to school.*~~

- You can often put time expressions at the beginning of the sentence, too. The meaning doesn't change.
  In June we're going to the Alps. OR *We're going to the Alps in June.*

Verb patterns (1)

Test it ✔

1 Find and correct the mistakes in the sentences.

Nicola thinks ~~to read~~ is a waste of time. reading

- **a** When I drove past your house I saw ten birds sit on the roof. ....
- **b** Suddenly, we heard a girl to scream. ....
- **c** Did you notice Jane staring at Simon last night? ....
- **d** We're going surfing in Cornwall next summer. ....
- **e** Leo loves tennising. ....
- **f** Jogging is a popular pastime. ....
- **g** To go shopping is what Jenny likes most of all. ....
- **h** We saw the postman fall off his bike but he was OK. ....
- **i** To see you again is the best thing that's happened to me for years. ....
- **j** One of Tim's worst habits is singing in the bath. ....

2 Write the *-ing* form, base form or the infinitive to complete the sentences.

I heard Carol tell (tell) a joke. Nobody laughed.

- **a** We saw a strange man .... (stand) outside the bank.
- **b** I suddenly felt a sharp pain .... (go) through my leg.
- **c** .... (practise) yoga is supposed to make you feel calm.
- **d** I'm listening to my favourite actor .... (speak) on the radio.
- **e** .... (keep) fit is good for your health and it makes you feel happier, too.
- **f** He saw the woman .... (get) out of the car and run off.
- **g** Jay hates .... (smoke) but he can't give it up.
- **h** Nick and Jeff are going .... (climb) next weekend.
- **i** We watched the people .... (dance) in the street – it was great fun.
- **j** Do you enjoy .... (play) squash?

☐ 20

GO to page 52 and check your answers.

Test it again ✓

1 Circle the best option, A or B.

Phil goes .... every weekend.
A to hike (**B**) hiking

a .... is good fun. I enjoy it.
A To cook **B** Cooking

b Steve loves ....
A playing football **B** footballing

c He heard the dog .... just before it bit Charlie.
A growl **B** to growl

d .... golf is incredibly boring in my opinion.
A Playing **B** To play

e I noticed a small rabbit .... by the side of the road.
A lie **B** lying

f .... happy is more important than anything else in life.
A Feel **B** Feeling

g .... every day makes him feel better.
A Running **B** Run

h They saw Peter .... the flowers in the bin and walk off.
A to throw **B** throw

i I heard someone .... loudly in the room next door.
A snoring **B** to snore

j Andrew and Jo both love ....
A marathoning **B** running marathons

k We watched the children .... on the beach.
A playing **B** to play

2 Choose the best caption for the cartoon.

I wish I were you. Move house is so stressful!
I wish I were you. Moving house is so stressful!
I wish I were you. To move house is so stressful!

| | 12 |

Fix it

Answers to Test it

Check your answers. Wrong answer? Read the right Fix it note to find out why.

1	•	~~to read~~	reading	→ A
	a	~~sit~~	sitting	→ D
	b	~~to scream~~	scream	→ C
	c	correct		→ D
	d	correct		→ A
	e	~~tennising~~	playing tennis	→ B
	f	correct		→ A
	g	~~To go~~	Going	→ A
	h	correct		→ C
	i	~~To see~~	Seeing	→ A
	j	correct		→ A

2	•	tell	→ C
	a	standing	→ D
	b	go	→ C
	c	Practising	→ A
	d	speaking	→ D
	e	Keeping	→ A
	f	get	→ C
	g	smoking	→ A
	h	climbing	→ A
	i	dancing	→ D
	j	playing	→ A

Now go to page 51. Test yourself again.

Answers to Test it again

1	a B	b A	c A	d A
	e B	f B	g A	h B
	i A	j B	k A	

2 I wish I were you. Moving house is so stressful!

Fix it notes

A

Use an *-ing* form (not an infinitive) as the subject or object of a sentence.

B

Make an *-ing* form from a verb. Don't make an *-ing* form from a noun.

C

After the verbs *feel, hear, notice, see, watch* + object, use the base form of the verb if the action is finished before you stop feeling, hearing, etc.

D

After the verbs *feel, hear, notice, see, watch* + object, use the *-ing* form if the action isn't finished before you stop feeling, hearing, etc.

For more information, see the Review page opposite.

Review

Verb patterns (1)

The *-ing* form as subject or object

- You can use the *-ing* form of a verb as the subject or object of a sentence. It behaves like a noun.
  Swimming is good for you. NOT ~~*To swim is good for you.*~~
  I like swimming.
  Be careful! You can't make an *-ing* form out of a noun.
  I like playing tennis. NOT ~~*I like tennising.*~~

Go

- You often use *go* + *-ing* form to talk about sports and leisure.
  Tony and I are going walking in the Alps next month.
  We're all going clubbing tonight. Do you want to come?

  Note that you don't normally use *to go* at the beginning of a sentence.
  Running is very important to David.
  NOT ~~*To go running is very important to David.*~~

Verbs + object + *-ing* form or base form

- After certain verbs, e.g. *feel, hear, notice, see, watch* + object you can use the base form. You use the base form when the action you're talking about is completed.
  I heard the door slam.
  Helen saw Stephen pick up the letter and throw it in the bin.

- You use the *-ing* form after *feel, hear, notice,* etc. + object when the action you're talking about isn't completed.
  We watched tourists floating in the Dead Sea.
  I noticed a monkey swinging through the trees.
  The witness saw a man standing on the corner.
  NOT ~~*The witness saw a man stand on the corner.*~~

Verb patterns (2)

Test it ✔

1 Tick the best sentence in each group.

Fergus is good at to cook. ☐
Fergus is good at cooking. ☑
Fergus is good at cook. ☐

a They're delighted to be here. ☐
b They're delighted be here. ☐
c They're delighted being here. ☐

d Apparently, there's a plan knocking that house down. ☐
e Apparently, there's a plan to knock that house down. ☐
f Apparently, there's a plan knock that house down. ☐

g Charlotte has no hope getting the job she wants. ☐
h Charlotte has no hope to get the job she wants. ☐
i Charlotte has no hope of getting the job she wants. ☐

j Of course I'm happy for you to use my car. ☐
k Of course I'm happy for you using my car. ☐
l Of course I'm happy you to use my car. ☐

m Matthew is ashamed of to cheat in the exam. ☐
n Matthew is ashamed of cheating in the exam. ☐
o Matthew is ashamed of cheat in the exam. ☐

2 Write complete sentences. Use the *-ing* form or infinitive of the verbs in brackets. Add *for* where necessary.

Roast lamb is easy and tastes wonderful. (cook) *easy to cook*

a It'll be a good opportunity us the schedule. (discuss) ....

b It's not unusual people nervous in an interview. (feel) ....

c Pete was shocked about the accident. (hear) ....

d You've got plenty of time for the test. (revise) ....

e Are you interested in about my life? (hear) ....

f The idea of house terrifies me. (move) ....

g Oh, come on! There's no need about it. (cry) ....

h Johnny had a dream of famous but he never was. (be) ....

i I have no desire pressure on you. (put) ....

j It's hard him how you feel. (imagine) ....

☐ 15

GO to page 56 and check your answers.

Test it again ✓

1 Circle the best option.

Caroline has dreams of become/to become/(becoming) an astronaut.

- **a** It's impossible for you to understand/understand/understanding the problem.
- **b** Nick seemed very pleased seeing/see/to see Cathy.
- **c** I'm sure Vic's guilty of steal/stealing/to steal the money.
- **d** Late spring is a very good time to go/go/going to Italy.
- **e** Jo's bored of hearing/hear/to hear your silly jokes.
- **f** I'm delighted to accept/accepting/accept your offer.
- **g** They had great difficulty in persuading/persuade/to pursuade us to go.
- **h** Let's make a decision to move/moving/move house soon.
- **i** That wasn't a very nice thing for her saying/say/to say.
- **j** Are you good at play/to play/playing the saxophone?

2 Find and correct the mistakes in the speech bubbles.

Weddings are great occasions for meeting old friends.
correct

a It's good people to eat fruit and vegetables.
....

b He can't stand the thought of dying.
....

c Don't worry! It's normal feeling scared of flying.
....

d There's no need to leave yet.
....

e There's no need you go until tomorrow.
....

f Do you know what? I'm completely fed up with to be here.
....

g We're both interested in finding out more about Central Asia.
....

h The thought of to marry you is heaven!
....

i I look forward to seeing your holiday photos.
....

j I'm relieved to know the truth at last.
....

| /20 |

Fix it

Answers to Test it

Check your answers. Wrong answer? Read the right Fix it note to find out why.

1 The best sentences are:

• → B	i → D
a → A	j → E
e → C	n → B

2
- • easy to cook → A
- a for us to discuss → E
- b for people to feel → E
- c shocked to hear → A
- d time to revise → C
- e interested in hearing → B
- f idea of moving → D
- g no need to cry → C
- h dream of being → D
- i no desire to put → C
- j for him to imagine → E

Now go to page 55. Test yourself again.

Answers to Test it again

1
- a to understand
- b to see
- c stealing
- d to go
- e hearing
- f to accept
- g persuading
- h to move
- i to say
- j playing

2

a ~~good people~~	good for people
b correct	
c ~~feeling~~	to feel
d correct	
e ~~need you go~~	need for you to go
f ~~to be~~	being
g correct	
h ~~to marry~~	marrying
i correct	
j correct	

Fix it notes

A

Use the infinitive (not the base form of the verb or the *-ing* form) after an adjective.

B

Use the *-ing* form (not the infinitive or the base form of the verb) if a preposition follows an adjective.

C

Use the infinitive (not the base form of the verb or the *-ing* form) after some nouns, e.g. *plan, opportunity, time, need, desire.*

D

Use the *-ing* form (not the infinitive or the base form) after some nouns + preposition, e.g. *hope of, idea of, dream of.*

E

Use *for* if you put an object between an adjective or a noun and the infinitive.

For more information, see the Review page opposite.

i Review

Verb patterns (2)

Adjective + infinitive or *-ing* form

- You can often use the infinitive after an adjective. You don't use the *-ing* form or the base form of the verb.
  I'm glad to see you. NOT ~~*I'm glad seeing you.*~~ NOT ~~*I'm glad see you.*~~
  We were shocked to hear the terrible news.
  NOT ~~*...hear/hearing the terrible news.*~~

- You use the *-ing* form when there's a preposition after an adjective, e.g. *bored with, excited about, good at, guilty of, interested in, pleased about.* (See the list on page 86.)
  He's good at swimming. NOT ~~*He's good at to swim.*~~
  NOT ~~*He's good at swim.*~~
  Clara's bored with playing tennis. *He was interested in learning all about her.*

Noun + infinitive or *-ing* form

- After some nouns, e.g. *decision, need, time, wish,* you use an infinitive (not an *-ing* form or the base form of the verb). (See the list on page 86.)
  There's a plan to build a motorway. NOT ~~*There's a plan building a motorway.*~~
  There's no need to go. NOT ~~*There's no need go.*~~
  NOT ~~*There's no need going.*~~

- You use the *-ing* form when there's a preposition after a noun, e.g. *difficulty in, hope of, idea of, thought of.* (See the list on page 86.)
  We've no hope of finding survivors. NOT ~~*We've no hope to find survivors.*~~
  I hate the idea of getting married. *John had difficulty in finding a hotel.*

Adjective or noun + *for* + object + infinitive

- If you want to put an object between an adjective or a noun and an infinitive, you must use *for.*
  I'm happy for you to use my house while I'm away.
  NOT ~~*I'm happy you to use...*~~
  The party will be a good opportunity for students to meet each other.

Verb patterns (3)

Test it ✔

1 Find and correct five mistakes in the sentences.

I found the cat ~~to eat~~ the salmon. *eating*

a She advised me seeing the manager. ....

b Mr Oliver stopped the children running across the road. ....

c He asked how spelling my name. ....

d I really don't know what to do. ....

e It was nice that Frank invited Ben to go on holiday. ....

f Ask the teacher what do next, please. ....

g My parents encouraged me becoming a solicitor. ....

h We discovered the men to break into the house. ....

i Do you know where to buy cheap software? ....

j Anthony reminded me to sign the cheque. ....

2 Complete the sentences. Use the correct form of the words in brackets.

Has Viv decided which film *to see* (see)?

a Malcolm Smith taught me .... (read) Ancient Greek.

b Please ask the agent when .... (book) the tickets.

c George dislikes animals .... (be) treated badly.

d Will you allow us .... (stay) up and watch the film?

e The woman asked us how .... (get) to the station.

f I want to know what .... (do) in this situation.

g Jude was embarrassed because the examiner caught her .... (cheat).

h No one can stop me .... (feel) the way I do.

i Andrew showed us how .... (frame) a picture.

j Let's ask the information centre where .... (eat).

| |20

GO to page 60 and check your answers.

Test it again ✓

1 Circle the best option, A or B.

Kath wouldn't allow her children .... with toy guns.
(**A**) to play **B** playing

a It was dangerous, but no one could stop John .... in the river.
A swim **B** swimming

b Edward didn't ask Lucy .... to his wedding.
A going **B** to go

c Do you know how .... 'onomatopeia'?
A to pronounce **B** pronouncing

d I'm not happy! I caught my boyfriend .... with another woman!
A to flirt **B** flirting

e Why don't you ask someone where .... in Barcelona?
A staying **B** to stay

f I dislike people .... at me. It's just not nice.
A to laugh **B** laughing

g Ask your mum how .... your homework. I don't know!
A to do **B** do

h Sylvia wanted me .... her my poems but I refused.
A to show **B** showing

i The policeman ordered us .... out of the car.
A getting **B** to get

j I found the dog .... my favourite book.
A chewing **B** chew

2 Find and correct the mistakes in the headlines.

Famous politician caught ~~to run~~ from crime scene. *running*

a Prime Minister helps pensioners to keep warm in winter. ....

b Teenagers prefer their parents staying away from school discos. ....

c Do it now! Find out how losing weight the safe, quick way! ....

d Actor encourages young talent to apply for film roles. ....

e 'I don't know what doing with all my money,' claims pop idol. ....

f Ministers want to get young homeless people off the streets. ....

g 'My parents stopped me to get married to the man I love,' says Norma-Jean. ....

h Agents advise house owners selling now while interest rates are low. ....

i 'I begged him not to go!' celebrity tells the nation. Read it all inside. ....

j Need cash? Find out where to get the best deals! ....

[ ] / 20

Fix it

Answers to Test it

Check your answers. Wrong answer? Read the right Fix it note to find out why.

1

•	~~to eat~~	eating	→ B
a	~~seeing~~	to see	→ A
b	correct		→ B
c	~~spelling~~	to spell	→ C
d	correct		→ C
e	correct		→ A
f	~~do~~	to do	→ C
g	~~becoming~~	to become	→ A
h	~~to break~~	breaking	→ B
i	correct		→ C
j	correct		→ A

2

•	to see	→ C
a	to read	→ A
b	to book	→ C
c	being	→ B
d	to stay	→ A
e	to get	→ C
f	to do	→ C
g	cheating	→ B
h	feeling	→ B
i	to frame	→ C
j	to eat	→ C

Now go to page 59. Test yourself again.

Answers to Test it again

1 **a** B **b** B **c** A **d** B **e** B
f B **g** A **h** A **i** B **j** A

2

a	correct	
b	~~staying~~	to stay
c	~~losing~~	to lose
d	correct	
e	~~doing~~	to do
f	correct	
g	~~to get~~	getting
h	~~selling~~	to sell
i	correct	
j	correct	

Fix it notes

A

Use object + infinitive (not *-ing* form) after certain verbs, e.g. *advise, allow, encourage, invite, remind, teach*.

B

Use object + *-ing* form after certain verbs, e.g. *catch* (= discover), *discover, dislike, stop*.

C

Use a question word + infinitive (not the base form of the verb or an *-ing* form), in reported speech and questions inside questions.

For more information, see the Review page opposite.

Review

Verb patterns (3)

Verb + object + infinitive or *-ing* form

- You use object + infinitive (not an *-ing* form) after certain verbs, e.g. *advise, allow, ask, encourage, invite, order, permit, persuade, prefer, remind, teach, want.* (See the list on page 87.)
  Mum allowed us to stay up late. NOT ~~*… staying up late.*~~
  She persuaded him to marry her. NOT ~~*… marrying her.*~~

- You use object + an *-ing* form (not an infinitive) after *catch* (= discover), *discover, dislike, find, stop,* etc. (See the list on page 87.)
  The teacher caught them copying. NOT ~~*The teacher caught them to copy.*~~
  They stopped her getting married. NOT ~~*They stopped her to get married.*~~

Question word + infinitive

- You often use a question word + infinitive (not the base form of the verb or an *-ing* form), especially in reported speech and questions inside questions. (For more information on embedded questions see page 77.)
  I didn't know where to go. NOT ~~*I didn't know where go.*~~
  I asked her how to spell it. NOT ~~*I asked her how spelling it.*~~
  Find out what to do next. NOT ~~*Find out what doing next.*~~

  Note: The only question word you can't put an infinitive after is *why*.

Contrast and connection

Test it ✔

1 Tick the correct sentence in each pair.

	In spite of it's difficult, I love my job.	☐
	In spite of the fact that it's difficult, I love my job.	☑
a	It's late. It's also getting dark.	☐
b	It's late. It's getting also dark.	☐
c	Lisa's a good driver, she hasn't though got a car.	☐
d	Lisa's a good driver, though she hasn't got a car.	☐
e	Although I got up early, it was a holiday.	☐
f	I got up early, it was a holiday although.	☐
g	I'm tired. I'm hungry as well.	☐
h	I'm tired. As well I'm hungry.	☐
i	I saw Sonia in the restaurant and David was there too.	☐
j	I saw Sonia in the restaurant and too David was there.	☐
k	Even although I was careful, I broke the vase.	☐
l	Even though I was careful, I broke the vase.	☐
m	As well as the cost, there's the problem of noise.	☐
n	There's the problem of noise, the cost as well as.	☐
o	I think we should still go camping, in spite of the bad weather.	☐
p	I think we should still go camping, even in spite of the bad weather.	☐
q	They bought a new car even though they couldn't afford it.	☐
r	They bought a new car, they couldn't afford it even though.	☐
s	In spite of feeling ill, Ann went to work.	☐
t	In spite of feel ill, Ann went to work.	☐

2 Circle the best option.

Even though/Even although Arsenal lost, it was a good match.

a There's a coffee shop in the hotel and it as well/also has a restaurant.
b I had another burger, even although/though I wasn't hungry.
c It's cold and windy in the North. It also/too snows a lot.
d Though/In spite of her shyness, she has many friends.
e Jenny's travelled in India. As well as that/Too, she's been to China.
f That boy's a brilliant dancer. He sings very well too/as well as.
g In spite of she went/the fact that she went to bed early, Emma woke up late.
h Maldini is a film director. He also is/'s also a good actor.
i My boyfriend likes football, though/in spite of I think it's really boring.
j Sugar can make you fat, and it's bad for your teeth as well/as well as.

☐ 20

GO to page 64 and check your answers.

Test it again ✓

1 Complete the music review. Use one word in each space.

also ~~*although*~~ *as* *as well as* *even* *in spite of* *though* (x2) *too*

Although .... it's taken two years to produce, it has been worth the wait. **Mirror image** *is Jay's best album since the band split up, and is* [a] *........................ the best of the albums that the ex-band-members have produced.* [b] *........................ some great new songs, there are some old favourites,* [c] *........................ perhaps a few of these now sound a bit out-of-date.* [d] *........................ this, the CD sounds very fresh, and contains a few surprises,* [e] *........................ well. Jay's piano solo on* **Clouds**, *for instance, is superb,* [f] *........................ though he only recently learnt to play. Jay's voice on this track is strong,* [g] *........................ . It's powerful throughout the album, in fact,* [h] *........................ some say he sounds better live.*

2 Rewrite the sentences, using a suitable connector. Keep the same meaning.

Eric loves music and poetry.
Eric loves music and he likes poetry *too/as well* .

a Ricky teaches and also writes books.
Ricky teaches. .... that, he writes books.

b I love skiing, but I'm not very good at it.
Even .... I love skiing, I'm not very good at it.

c Even though the sun has set, it's still warm.
In spite of .... the sun has set, it's still warm.

d I made lunch and did the washing up, too.
.... making lunch, I did the washing up.

e It was raining, but we went for a walk anyway.
.... though it was raining, we went for a walk.

f In spite of reading it twice, I didn't understand it.
.... that I read it twice, I didn't understand it.

g Helen reads a lot. She often goes to the theatre, too.
Helen often goes to the theatre and she .... reads a lot.

h We both like swimming and snorkelling.
We like swimming and we enjoy snorkelling ....

i Karen's nice to Jake in spite of the fact that she doesn't like him much.
.... Karen's nice to Jake, she doesn't like him much.

j My dog is very gentle. He's also very loyal.
.... being gentle, my dog's very loyal.

☐ 18

Fix it

Answers to Test it

Check your answers. Wrong answer? Read the right Fix it note to find out why.

1 The correct sentences are:

- • → D
- a → A
- d → C
- e → C
- g → A
- i → A
- l → E
- m → B
- o → E
- q → C
- s → D

2
- • Even though → E
- a also → A
- b though → E
- c also → A
- d In spite of → C, D
- e As well as that → A, B
- f too → A, B
- g the fact that she went → D
- h 's also → A
- i though → C, D
- j as well → A, B

Now go to page 63. Test yourself again.

Answers to Test it again

1
- a also
- b As well as
- c though
- d In spite of
- e as
- f even
- g too
- h though

2
- a As well as
- b though
- c the fact (that)
- d As well as
- e Even
- f In spite of the fact
- g also
- h too/as well
- i Although/Though
- j As well as

Fix it notes

A

Put *as well* or *too* at the end of a sentence. *Also* goes before the main verb but after *be*.

B

Put *as well as (that)* at the beginning or in the middle of a sentence (not at the end).

C

Use *although, though* or *even though* with subject + verb. Put them at the beginning of the correct part of the sentence.

D

Use *in spite of* only before a noun or before an *-ing* form of a verb. Add *the fact (that)* before other verb forms.

E

Don't put *even* before *although* or *in spite of.*

For more information, see the Review page opposite.

Review

Contrast and connection

Also, as well, too

- You put *also* before the main verb in a sentence. But you must put it after (not before) the verb *be.*
  We produce fruit here and we also grow vegetables.
  She was kind and she was also generous. NOT ~~*... she also was generous.*~~
  There's a hotel in the village. There's also a café and a restaurant.

- You usually put *as well* and *too* at the end of a sentence.
  You can see the person on the screen and talk to them as well/too.
  NOT ~~*... and as well talk to them/too talk to them.*~~

As well as

- You can begin a sentence with *as well as*, but only before a noun or the *-ing* form of a verb. You don't use *as well as* at the end of a sentence.
  As well as a TV, there's a DVD. *As well as having a TV, he's got a DVD.*
  Dogs need water as well as food. NOT ~~*... water and food as well as.*~~

Although, though and *even though*

- You use *although, though* and *even though* with subject + verb. *Though* is less formal than *although*. You use *even though* to make what you're saying sound stronger. Often the information that comes after *although, though* and *even though* makes the idea in the other part of the sentence seem surprising.
  The plants grew well, even though she rarely watered them.
  OR *Even though she rarely watered them, the plants grew well.*
  (It was surprising that the plants grew well.)

In spite of

- You use *in spite* of like *although*. It goes before a noun or the *-ing* form of a verb. You add *the fact (that)* before other verb forms.
  In spite of his size, the rugby player could run fast.
  In spite of feeling sleepy, Paul watched the whole film.
  In spite of the fact that I usually lose, I enjoy playing cards.
  NOT ~~*In spite of I usually lose ...*~~

- You can reverse the order of the clauses. The meaning doesn't change.
  In spite of his size, the rugby player could run fast.
  OR *The rugby player could run fast, in spite of his size.*

Purpose

Test it ✔

1 Find and correct the mistakes in the sentences.

Matt set off at 6.00 a.m. to make sure ~~not to be late~~.
he wasn't late

a Carol went to the bank for to get some cash.
....

b Jeff studied hard to make sure he passed the exam.
....

c I went outside that I could get some fresh air.
....

d We must use cars less to reduce pollution.
....

e I'm saving to a new DVD player.
....

f I always take a map so that I don't get lost.
....

g Paula runs every day in order get fit.
....

h He aimed carefully in order not to miss the target.
....

i Superglue is useful for fix broken plastic.
....

j I wrote it down so that not to forget it.
....

2 Complete the sentences. Use each word or expression twice.

for *in order to* *so that* *to make* *to make sure*

I had to shout *so that* everyone could hear me.

a Jackie went to Warsaw .... learn Polish.
b When you're abroad, internet cafés are useful .... sending emails.
c Look in the fridge .... we have enough food for everyone.
d The Oscar winner stood up .... a speech to everyone.
e He bought lots of lottery tickets .... he would have a better chance of winning.
f Please have the correct money ready .... avoid delays.
g You need olive oil .... a good salad dressing.
h I always use a red pen .... correcting my mistakes.
i Have you counted the chairs .... we have enough?
j Come to my new house .... I can show you around.

☐ 20

GO to page 68 and check your answers.

Test it again ✔

1 Circle the best option.

SUE Do you have a reason to/(for) shouting at me?
TOM You went out [a] to/for to see Mark last night, didn't you?
SUE No, I didn't. I went out [b] in order for/for a coffee with some friends, that's all. Anyway, I left early [c] not to/so I didn't miss the bus home. That's when I phoned you. I borrowed someone's phone [d] to call/for calling you because the battery in mine was low. And I phoned [e] in order to/so you'd know I was thinking about you, as I always do.
TOM You're only saying that [f] so I don't/so I not get angry with you.
SUE No, no. It's true. It's [g] for to stop/to stop you getting the wrong idea.
TOM Well, I'm going to call that number back now. Just [h] for making sure/ to make sure you're telling me the truth.
SUE Why don't you trust me? I didn't go on holiday with my friends so that [i] you wouldn't/you not get jealous. I'm saving all my money for [j] our wedding/to get married, but now I might change my mind.
TOM OK, I believe you. I'm sorry.
SUE Well, make sure [k] to not /you don't do it again!

2 Choose the best caption for the cartoon.

He moved quietly in order to not wake it up.
He moved quietly so that he didn't wake it up.
He moved quietly for not waking it up.

| | 12 |

Fix it

Answers to Test it

Check your answers. Wrong answer? Read the right Fix it note to find out why.

1
- • ~~not to be late~~ he wasn't late → D
- a ~~for to get~~ to get → A
- b correct → D
- c ~~that~~ so that → C
- d correct → A
- e ~~to~~ for → E
- f correct → C
- g ~~in order~~ in order to → B
- h correct → B
- i ~~for fix~~ for fixing → E
- j ~~so that not to~~ so that I didn't/wouldn't → C

2
- • so that → C
- a in order to → B
- b for → E
- c to make sure → D
- d to make → A
- e so that → C
- f in order to → B
- g to make → A
- h for → E
- i to make sure → D
- j so that → C

Now go to page 67. Test yourself again.

Answers to Test it again

1
- a to
- b for
- c so I didn't
- d to call
- e so
- f so I don't
- g to stop
- h to make sure
- i you wouldn't
- j our wedding
- k you don't

2 He moved quietly so that he didn't wake it up.

Fix it notes

A

Use *to* + base form of the verb to say why someone does something.

B

Use *in order to* + base form of the verb to say why someone does something. The negative is *in order not to* + base form of the verb.

C

Use *so (that)* + a modal verb. In the negative, use a form of the verb *do* or a modal verb, e.g. *... so (that) I didn't ...*, *... so (that) he wouldn't ....*

D

Use subject + verb after *to make sure (that)*.

E

Use *for* before a noun or before the *-ing* form of the verb.

For more information, see the Review page opposite.

Review

Purpose

To

- You can use *to* + base form of the verb to say why someone does something. You use *in order not to* as the negative form.
  We sat down to eat. *He went back to the office to read the report.*
  The driver braked in order not to crash. NOT ~~*The driver braked, not to crash.*~~
  NOT ~~*The driver braked, to not crash.*~~

In order to

- You can also use *in order to* + base form of the verb to say why someone does something. This is more formal than *to* + base form of the verb. You use *in order not to* as the negative form.
  He ran to save time. (informal) *He ran in order to save time.* (formal)
  Keep quiet, in order not to wake the baby.
  NOT ~~*Keep quiet, not in order to wake the baby.*~~

So (that)

- You usually use *so* or *so that* with a modal verb such as *can*, *will*, etc.
  I shouted so that they could hear me. NOT ~~*I shouted so that they heard me.*~~
- You can use *will* or the present simple after *so (that)* to talk about the future.
  Take your passport so they'll let you in. OR *... so they let you in.*
- In the negative, you use a modal verb or a form of the verb *do*.
  She hid the mark so people wouldn't notice.
  Wear a hat so that you don't get cold. NOT ~~*Wear a hat so that not get cold.*~~

Make sure (that)

- You can use *to make sure (that)* to say that someone is determined to do something.
  They trained hard to make sure they won. NOT ~~*... to make sure to win.*~~
- You make the negative by using *to make sure (that)* + *do* + *not*.
  I got there early to make sure I didn't miss it.
  NOT ~~*... not to make sure I missed it.*~~

For

- You can use *for* to say why someone does something or what you use something for, but only before a noun or an *-ing* form.
  I'm studying for an exam. NOT ~~*I'm studying for to take an exam.*~~
  A lawnmower is for cutting grass. NOT ~~*A lawnmower is for to cut grass.*~~

Result and reason

Test it ✓

1 Tick the correct sentence in each pair.

	The film is good because I've seen it twice.	☐
	The film is good so I've seen it twice.	☑
a	Jo phoned the company because of he wanted a job.	☐
b	Jo phoned the company because he wanted a job.	☐
c	It was such a good book that I read it in a day.	☐
d	It was a such good book that I read it in a day.	☐
e	The bus was late, so Lisse walked to work.	☐
f	The bus was late, so that Lisse walked to work.	☐
g	Gina was too much busy to have lunch.	☐
h	Gina was much too busy to have lunch.	☐
i	Steve drove fast so that he crashed.	☐
j	Steve drove so fast that he crashed.	☐
k	Take my number in case you need to call me.	☐
l	Take my number in case you would need to call me.	☐
m	It was such dark that we couldn't see anything.	☐
n	It was so dark that we couldn't see anything.	☐
o	The fruit is ripe enough to eat now.	☐
p	The fruit is enough ripe to eat now.	☐

2 Circle the best option.

It's (much too)/too much cold to play tennis today.

- **a** I couldn't sleep because/because of the noise.
- **b** The bus goes such/so slowly that it's quicker on foot.
- **c** Clive was too/too much tired to work any more.
- **d** Let's take some water in case we'll be/we're thirsty later.
- **e** There was such a/a such terrible storm that the ship sank.
- **f** The traffic lights turned green, because/so the cars started moving.
- **g** Sophie's not enough tall/not tall enough to be a model.
- **h** Pam wanted to learn Spanish, so/so that she spent a year in Madrid.
- **i** I feel much happier because/because of you!
- **j** Don't touch that wire in case you/you'll get an electric shock.

☐ 18

GO to page 72 and check your answers.

Test it again ✓

1 Complete the sentences. Keep the same meaning.

Katy's phone was off so I left a message.
I left a message *because Katy's phone was off* .

a It's too cold to swim.
It's not warm ....

b She bought that jacket because it was half price.
That jacket was half price, ...

c It's such a cold day that I can't believe it.
It's so ....

d Take some food – you might get hungry.
Take some food in case ....

e The film was so good that I saw it twice.
It was such .... that I saw it twice.

f This car isn't big enough for our family.
This car is too ....

g I'll stay at home in case she phones later.
I'll stay at home because ....

h Nick wrote such a good essay that he won the competition.
Nick won the competition because .... a good essay.

i It was raining, so they postponed the match.
They postponed the match .... the rain.

j It was extremely hot, so no one stayed on the beach.
It was .... to stay on the beach.

2 Complete the sentences. Use the words given and any other words you need from the first sentence.

You look too young to be a grandmother. **enough**
You don't look old *enough to be a* grandmother.

a That shop is so expensive that I never go there. **such**
It's .... shop that I never go there.

b Because of the snow and ice, the airport was closed. **so**
There was snow and ice, ... closed.

c It's so late that there's no point in going to bed. **too**
It's .... to go to bed.

d You might get home late so take a key with you. **in case**
Take a key with you .... home late.

e The problem is too difficult for me to solve. **that**
The problem is .... I can't solve it.

f Teresa loves Egypt so she often goes there. **because**
Teresa often goes to Egypt .... it.

| | 16 |

Fix it

Answers to Test it

Check your answers. Wrong answer? Read the right Fix it note to find out why.

1 The correct sentences are:

● → A	j → A
b → D	k → E
c → C	n → B
e → A	o → G
h → F	

2

● much too	→ F
a because of	→ D
b so	→ B
c too	→ F
d we're	→ E
e such a	→ C
f so	→ A
g not tall enough	→ G
h so	→ A
i because of	→ D
j you	→ E

Now go to page 71. Test yourself again.

Answers to Test it again

1
- **a** enough to swim
- **b** so she bought it
- **c** cold (that) I can't believe it
- **d** you get hungry
- **e** a good film
- **f** small for our family
- **g** she might phone later
- **h** he wrote/had written such
- **i** because of
- **j** too hot

2
- **a** such an expensive
- **b** so the airport was
- **c** too late
- **d** in case you get
- **e** so difficult that
- **f** because she loves

Fix it notes

A

Put *so* (not *so that* or *because*), after a reason and before a result.

B

Use *so* (not *such*) before an adjective or adverb on its own.

C

Use *such* before a noun or adjective + noun. If there's an article (*a* or *an*), put it after *such*.

D

Use *because* before subject + verb. Use *because of* before a noun or pronoun.

E

Use the present simple after *in case* to talk about future possibility.

F

Use *too* + adjective/adverb + infinitive. You can say *much too* before an adjective/adverb, but not *too much*.

G

Use (*not* +) adjective/adverb + *enough* + infinitive.

For more information, see the Review page opposite.

Review

Result and reason

So and *such*

- You can use *so* to say why something happens.
  Colin was tired, so he went home. (He was tired. Because of that he went home.)
  It was funny, so everyone laughed. (Because it was funny, everyone laughed.)

- You can also use *so ... (that)* or *such ... that* to say why something happens. You use *so* before an adjective or adverb. You use *such* before a noun or before an adjective + noun. You put *a* or *an* after (not before) *such* with singular countable nouns.
  The water was so cold it froze. *It was such a shock that he cried.*
  He was such a good player that he won.
  They were such good doctors that they saved the man's life.

Because (of) and *in case*

- You use *because* to give a reason for something. You put it before a subject + verb. You use *because of* before a noun or a pronoun.
  She smiled because she had done it. *I wore a hat because of the hot sun.*
  Jan lost a lot of money because of him.

- You can use *in case* + present simple (not *will*) to talk about a future possibility. The future possibility gives you a reason for doing something now, in the present.
  Take a book in case you have to wait. (You might have to wait.)
  NOT ~~*Take a book in case you'll have to wait.*~~
  Be careful! *In case* doesn't mean 'if'.
  Come to my house if you want to. NOT ~~*... in case you want to.*~~

- You can use *because* for future possibility, but only with a modal verb.
  Take an umbrella in case it rains. OR *Take an umbrella because it might rain.*

Too and *enough*

- You can use *too* + adjective/adverb + infinitive to say why something can or can't happen. You don't add words like *much* or *very*.
  He was too angry to speak. NOT ~~*He was too much angry ...*~~
  NOT ~~*He was too very angry ...*~~

- You can also use adjective/adverb + *enough* + infinitive to give reasons. In the negative, you put *not* before the adjective or adverb.
  She's old enough to vote now.
  It isn't hot enough to swim. NOT ~~*... enough hot to swim.*~~

Embedded questions and replies

Test it ✔

1 Find and correct five mistakes in the questions and replies.

Do you think Ruth will marry Rick? ~~I don't expect.~~
I don't expect so.

a Could you tell me where the post office is? No, sorry. I don't live here.
....

b Do you know why did Sue leave her job? No, I've no idea.
....

c Do you think the bus will come soon? I don't think.
....

d Do you have any idea how long I'll have to wait? Not long. Only a day or two.
....

e Can you tell me when is the meeting? I think it's ten o'clock on Tuesday.
....

f Do you think that Fred's team will win the match? I don't hope!
....

g Could you tell us how this works? Yes, certainly.
....

h Does anyone know why Pete isn't here? No. Sorry.
....

i Do you think we'll pass the exam? Yes, I suppose.
....

j Could you tell me what the time is? It's just after two.
....

2 Circle the best option.

Do you think can you/(you can) help me?

a Katy asked how old I was/was I.

b They wanted to know where the airport was/was the airport.

c Can you tell me where Paddy lives/does Paddy live?

d Gina asked how much was the flat/the flat was.

e Do you know why this makes/does this make a noise?

☐ 15

GO to page 76 and check your answers.

Test it again ✓

1 Complete the speech bubbles.

What shall we do?
Do you know *what we should do* ?

a What time is it?
Could you tell me .... ?

b Where's Helen?
Do you know .... ?

c When does the lesson start?
She wanted to know .... ?

d How far is Paris from here?
Could you tell me .... ?

e Did he get my email?
Do you think .... ?

f How much is this?
Could you tell us .... ?

g When can I see Jim?
Do you know .... ?

h How does this thing work?
Can you tell me .... ?

i Where are you going, Luke?
Fred wanted to know .... ?

j Why did he say that?
Do you know .... ?

2 Circle the correct option, A or B.

'Do you think the president was telling the truth?' 'I ....'
(**A**) don't suppose so **B** don't suppose

a George asked me ....
A where was my house **B** where my house was

b 'Can you fix it?' 'No, ...'
A I don't think so **B** I don't think

c Could you tell us .... ?
A when does it start **B** when it starts

d 'Do you think it's going to rain?' 'I ....'
A hope not **B** don't hope

e Can you show me .... ?
A where is the cathedral **B** where the cathedral is

☐ 15

Fix it

Answers to Test it

Check your answers. Wrong answer? Read the right Fix it note to find out why.

1
- • ~~I don't expect.~~ I don't expect so. → C
- **a** correct → A
- **b** ~~did Sue leave~~ Sue left → B
- **c** ~~I don't think.~~ I don't think so. → D
- **d** correct → A
- **e** ~~is the meeting~~ the meeting is → A
- **f** ~~I don't hope!~~ I hope not! → E
- **g** correct → B
- **h** correct → A
- **i** ~~I suppose.~~ I suppose so. → C
- **j** correct → A

2
- • you can → A
- **a** I was → A
- **b** the airport was → A
- **c** Paddy lives → B
- **d** the flat was → A
- **e** this makes → B

Now go to page 75. Test yourself again.

Answers to Test it again

1
- **a** what the time is/what time it is
- **b** where Helen is
- **c** when the lesson started
- **d** how far Paris is from here/how far it is to Paris from here
- **e** he got my email
- **f** how much this is
- **g** when I can see Jim
- **h** how this thing works
- **i** where Luke was going
- **j** why he said that

2 **a** B **b** A **c** B **d** A **e** B

Fix it notes

A

Put auxiliary verbs, e.g. *be*, and modal verbs, e.g. *will*, after (not before) the subject in a question inside a question.

B

Don't use *do*, *does* or *did* in a question inside a question.

C

When you answer a question inside a question positively with the verbs *think*, *hope*, *expect* and *suppose*, put *so* after the verb.

D

When you answer a question inside a question negatively with the verbs *think*, *expect* and *suppose*, put *so* after the verb.

E

When you answer a question inside a question negatively with the verb *hope*, put *not* after the verb.

For more information, see the Review page opposite.

Review

Embedded questions and replies

Embedded questions are questions that are hidden inside longer questions. For example, the question: 'Where's my jacket?' becomes '... where my jacket is' when it's inside the question 'Do you know ...?' When you ask people for information, you often use, 'Do you know ...?', 'Can/Could you tell me ...?', 'Do you think ...?', etc. When you use this kind of question, the word order changes.

There are two kinds of embedded question. There are embedded questions in reported speech. (*See Test it, Fix it: Verbs and Tenses Pre-intermediate* page 81, and *Test it, Fix it: Verbs and Tenses Intermediate* pages 41 and 45.) There are also embedded questions in polite question forms.

- When you use an embedded question, you put auxiliary and modal verbs after (not before) the subject.
  Where's Paddy? ➔ *Do you know where Paddy is?*
  When will we get there? ➔ *Can you tell me when we'll get there?*

- You don't use *do*, *does* or *did* in embedded questions.
  When does the news start? ➔ *Do you know when the news starts?*
  NOT ~~*... when does the news start?*~~

- You often answer embedded questions with the verbs *think*, *hope*, *expect* and *suppose*. When the answer is positive, you put *so* after the verb.
  'Do you think it'll be a nice day tomorrow?' 'Yes, I think so.' OR *'I hope so.'*
  'Can you tell me what the answer is?' 'Yes, I suppose so.' OR *'I expect so.'*

- When you answer an embedded question negatively with the verbs *think*, *expect* and *suppose*, you put *so* after the verb.
  'Do you think they'll win the match?' 'No, I don't think so'.
  OR *'I don't suppose so'.*
  OR *'I don't expect so.'*

- When you answer an embedded question negatively with the verb *hope*, you put *not* after the verb.
  'Do you think you'll fail the test?' 'I hope not!' NOT ~~*'I don't hope so.'*~~

Either ... or, neither ... nor, etc.

Test it ✔

1 Circle the best option, A or B.

Sue has three children. .... is a girl and the others are boys.
A Another (**B**) One

a Can you give me .... piece of paper, please?
A another **B** other

b She's .... rich nor famous, so no one's interested in her.
A not **B** neither

c You should take .... the 8.30 or the 8.45 train.
A either **B** neither

d I've got three sisters. One is married and .... are not.
A others **B** the others

e 'Sandra didn't tell me.' ....
A 'Me nor.' **B** 'Nor me.'

f I've got .... things to do at the moment.
A another **B** other

g You can have .... strawberries or melon.
A either **B** or

h 'I can't stand people who shout all the time.' ....
A 'Neither me.' **B** 'Me neither.'

i The cobra is poisonous but many .... snakes are harmless.
A other **B** others

j .... three people have died.
A Another **B** Other

2 Complete the sentences. Use the words below.

another (x2) *either* (x2) *or* *other*
others *neither* *nor* *the others* (x2)

Either .... eat your dinner or go to your room!

a Some people like oysters, but .... people hate them.
b Sheila has .... a big house nor a car, but she's happy.
c I go out one evening a week and spend all .... at home.
d Oh no, not .... problem!
e Kathy has two children and is expecting .... in June.
f I think I'll buy .... the white shirt or the blue one.
g Mike wanted to go, but .... wanted to stay.
h It's neither warm .... sunny at this time of year.
i Some months of the year have 30 days but .... have 31.
j That animal is probably either a fox .... a young wolf.

☐ 20

GO to page 80 and check your answers.

Test it again ✓

1 Circle the best option.

And now (another)/other chance to hear the weather forecast. The weather has changed little overnight, with no large falls in temperature [a] or/either in coastal [b] or/nor in inland areas. None of the main northern roads are closed. Of the mountain villages, one, San Fernando, is cut off by snow, but [c] other/the others remain open to traffic. This situation will continue for at least [d] another/other twelve hours. [e] Neither/None heavy rain [f] or/nor snow is expected, and there will not be any fog in mountain or coastal areas. Tomorrow, the north will remain cold, but [g] other/others areas will become warmer. It [h] will/won't be neither windy nor wet.

2 Write new sentences. Keep the same meaning.

Pete could win the award, but so could Liam.
Either *Liam or Pete* could win the award.

a He didn't smile. He didn't say anything.
He neither smiled .... anything.

b All the boys except one have gone.
One of the boys is still here, but .... have gone.

c Not all people like sport.
Some people like sport but .... don't.

d His name might be Bobby. It might also be Robbie.
His name is either ....

e I met three more people waiting outside.
I met another .... waiting outside.

f 'I don't think they saw me.' 'I don't think they saw me, either.'
'I don't think they saw me.' 'Nor ....'

g There wasn't any food and there was nothing to drink.
There was neither .... to drink.

| 15

Fix it

Answers to Test it

Check your answers. Wrong answer? Read the right Fix it note to find out why.

1
- • B → F
- a A → D
- b B → A
- c A → A
- d B → F
- e B → B
- f B → E
- g A → A
- h B → B
- i A → E
- j A → C

2
- • Either → A
- a other → E
- b neither → A
- c the others → F
- d another → C
- e another → C
- f either → A
- g the others → F
- h nor → A
- i others → E
- j or → A

Now go to page 79. Test yourself again.

Answers to Test it again

1
- a either
- b or
- c the others
- d another
- e Neither
- f nor
- g other
- h will

2
- a nor said
- b the others/the other boys
- c other people/others
- d Bobby or Robbie
- e three people
- f me
- g (any) food nor anything

Fix it notes

A

Use *either ... or* for two possibilities.
Use *neither ... nor* for the negative.
Don't say *either ... nor* or *neither ... or.*
Don't use *or ... or.*

B

Use *Nor me* or *Me neither* to agree with a negative statement (not *Me too*).

C

Use *another* on its own, with singular nouns or with a number + plural noun.

D

Use *another* (not *other*) to say 'an extra ...'.

E

Use *other* (not *others* and not *another*) with plural nouns.

F

Use *one* to talk about a single member of a group and *the other(s)* for the rest of the group.

For more information, see the Review page opposite.

Review

Either … or, neither … nor, etc.

Either … or, neither … nor

- You use *either … or* to talk about two possibilities.
  We can go either to Rome or Milan. NOT ~~*We can go or to Rome or Milan.*~~

- You use *neither … nor* for two negative facts.
  Neither he nor I slept. NOT ~~*Neither he or I slept.*~~

- You don't use negative verb forms with *neither … nor.*
  We neither ate nor drank. NOT ~~*We didn't neither eat nor drink.*~~

- You use *Nor me* or *Me neither* to agree with a negative comment.
  'Cricket doesn't interest me.' 'Nor me.' NOT ~~*'Me too.'*~~
  'I didn't go to work yesterday.' 'Me neither.' NOT ~~*'Nor I didn't.'*~~

Another/others, one … the other(s)

- You use *another* with a singular noun, or a number + plural noun.
  I've got another pen. OR *I've got another two pens.*
  NOT ~~*I've got another pens.*~~

- You use *another*, not *other*, to mean 'an extra …' or 'more'.
  I'd like another drink, please. NOT ~~*I'd like other drink, please.*~~

- You use *others* as a pronoun, but not as an adjective.
  Some birds sing but others don't.
  NOT ~~*Some birds sing but others birds don't.*~~

- You use *one* about a member of a group, and then *the other(s)* for the rest of the group.
  We saw two houses. One of them was attractive but the other was ugly.
  One person came outside but the others stayed in the house.

As and *like*

Test it ✔

1 Find and correct the mistakes in the sentences.

This chicken tastes as cardboard.
like ....

a My father works like a lawyer.
....

b As a girl, I lived in Brazil.
....

c I enjoy team sports such as basketball and hockey.
....

d We're having a party on Friday, like you know.
....

e Your handwriting is a lot like mine.
....

f That looks as a taxi coming now.
....

g Evergreen trees like pine and fir grow well here.
....

h Here, as in many other countries, people are hungry.
....

i Billy! Stop behaving as a clown and sit down.
....

j Apparently, I look as my mother.
....

2 Complete the sentences. Use *as* or *like*.

Ash believes in free trade, *as*.......... Johnstone does.

- **a** In an emergency, you can use a clean handkerchief .... a bandage.
- **b** Mr Burdon's house is so big it's .... a palace.
- **c** They sell newspapers such .... *The Guardian* and *The Independent* here.
- **d** .... I feared, my message arrived too late.
- **e** There was a sudden noise from the street, ... a bomb going off.
- **f** Speaking .... a doctor, my advice to you is to stop smoking now.
- **g** You must be extremely pleased with your exam results, ... we are.
- **h** Walking through the Atacama Desert is .... exploring the moon.
- **i** She was very ill .... a baby, but she seems fine now.
- **j** I don't want to be too thin, ... some of those models.

[ ] 20

GO to page 84 and check your answers.

Test it again ✓

1 Complete the sentences. Use *as* or *like*.

I'm worried that Joanne might fail her exams.
I hope Joanne doesn't fail her exams, ...as... I fear.

a Alan wants to be an electrical engineer.
Alan wants to work .... an electrical engineer.

b My two dogs look almost the same as one another.
My two dogs look .... one another.

c When she was a teenager, Carmen played a lot of sports.
Carmen played a lot of sports .... a teenager.

d Paddy writes things in the same way as Dad: untidily!
Paddy writes .... Dad: untidily!

e I've already explained that I haven't got any money.
I haven't got any money, ... I've already explained.

f Small cars, for example the Smart car, are easy to park.
It's easy to park small cars such .... the Smart car.

g If you haven't got a corkscrew, you can use a biro.
You can use a biro .... a corkscrew if you haven't got one.

h Sometimes Freddy looks very similar to an angel.
Sometimes Freddy looks .... an angel

i Tony is a teacher at St Paul's school.
Tony works .... a teacher at St Paul's school.

j This drink tastes very similar to pineapple juice.
This drink tastes .... pineapple juice.

2 Match a–k to 1–11. Add *as* or *like*.

a She likes visiting cities	**1** Penang and Java.	**a** ...11, like...
b Australia has some unusual animals,	**2** seeds.	**b** ....
c Jane is a teacher,	**3** I said before.	**c** ....
d Felicity enjoys playing tennis,	**4** koalas and emus.	**d** ....
e She's so funny, she looks	**5** lions and tigers.	**e** ....
f Before I became a writer, I worked	**6** her mother.	**f** ....
g Most plants begin life	**7** plastic.	**g** ....
h It really doesn't matter,	**8** a penguin.	**h** ....
i The food on planes tastes	**9** a trapeze artist.	**i** ....
j He enjoys exotic places such	**10** her mother used to.	**j** ....
k There are dangerous animals in the zoo, such	**11** Berlin and Vienna.	**k** ....

☐ 20

Fix it

Answers to Test it

Check your answers. Wrong answer?
Read the right Fix it note to find out why.

1
- • ~~as~~ like → A
- **a** ~~like~~ as → C
- **b** correct → D
- **c** correct → F
- **d** ~~like~~ as → E
- **e** correct → A
- **f** ~~as~~ like → A
- **g** correct → F
- **h** correct → B
- **i** ~~as~~ like → A
- **j** ~~as~~ like → A

2
- • as → B
- **a** as → C
- **b** like → A
- **c** as → F
- **d** As → E
- **e** like → A
- **f** as → D
- **g** as → B
- **h** like → A
- **i** as → D
- **j** like → A

Now go to page 83. Test yourself again.

Answers to Test it again

1
- **a** as
- **b** like
- **c** as
- **d** like
- **e** as
- **f** as
- **g** as
- **h** like
- **i** as
- **j** like

2
- **a** 11, like
- **b** 4, like
- **c** 6, like
- **d** 10, as
- **e** 8, like
- **f** 9, as
- **g** 2, as
- **h** 3, as
- **i** 7, like
- **j** 1, as
- **k** 5, as

Fix it notes

A

Use *like* (not *as*) before a noun or a pronoun to say that something is similar to something else.

B

Use *as* (not *like*) before subject + verb, or before a preposition, to say that something is similar to something else.

C

Use *as* (not *like*) for jobs and when you use something to do the job of something else.

D

Use *as* (not *like*) to mean 'in the role of' or 'when'.

E

You can use *as* (but not *like*) before subject + certain verbs, e.g. *know*, *fear*.

F

Use *like* or *such as* (not *as*) to give examples.

For more information, see the Review page opposite.

Review

As and *like*

Like

- You use *like* to say that something or someone is similar to something or someone else. It's a preposition, so it often goes before a noun or a pronoun.
  Christopher is like his father. *Samantha is a scientist, like me.*

- You use *like* after a verb of perception (e.g. *feel, look, seem, smell, sound, taste*) with a noun followed by the *-ing* form.
  That smells like milk burning. *It sounded like a baby crying.*

- You also use *like* before an *-ing* form when you're comparing one person or thing with someone or something else.
  Wearing these trainers is like walking on air.

- You use *like*, not *as*, to give examples, but you can also use *such as*.
  My brother hates green vegetables like sprouts and cabbage.
  That shop sells precious stones such as diamonds and rubies.

As

- *As* is a conjunction. You use it to talk about things that are similar. You only use it before a subject and verb, or before a preposition.
  I live by the river, as Joe does. *In the city, as on the coast, the traffic's heavy.*

- You use *as* for someone's job, or to say what you use something for.
  Marta works as a librarian. *Some people use the town square as a car park.*

- You use *as* to say that someone's job, age or role is important.
  As an engineer, he understood the dangers.
  (Because he was an engineer, he understood the dangers.)
  I often went there as a child. (I often went there when I was a child.)
  As a parent, her attitude to TV programmes has changed. (Now that she's a parent, her attitude to TV programmes has changed.)

  Note: Be careful! *As* and *like* don't mean the same thing.
  As a student, he has to do homework. (Because he's a student, he has to do homework.)
  Like a student, he has to do homework. (He's a teacher, but I'm comparing him to a student.)

- You can use *as* with verbs like *expect, fear, know* and *say*.
  I don't trust that man, as I've said many times before.
  As we hoped, the operation was a complete success.

Common structures with adjectives, nouns and verbs

Here are some lists of adjectives, nouns and verbs that you can use with *-ing* forms and infinitives.

Adjective + preposition + *-ing* form (See page 57.)

afraid of
amazed at
angry about/at
annoyed about/at
anxious about
ashamed of
aware of
awful about/at
bad at
bored with
brilliant at/for
capable of
clever at
content with
dependent on/upon
different from/to
disappointed about/at
excited about/at
famous for
fed up with
fond of
frightened of
good at/for
grateful for
guilty about/of
happy about/with
hopeless at
interested in
involved in
keen on
nervous about/of
pleased about/at/with
proud of
ready for
responsible for
satisfied with
scared of
sick of
sorry for/about
successful at/in
surprised at
terrible at/for
terrified of
tired of
used to
worried about
wrong about/with

Noun + preposition + *-ing* form (See page 57.)

advantage of/in
aim of/in
amazement at
anger about/at
annoyance about/at
anxiety about/over
apology for
awareness of
belief in
boredom of
chance of
danger of/in
difficulty in/of/with
dream of
effect of
excitement about/at/of
expense of/in
fear of
gratitude for
hope of
idea about/for/of
insistence on
intention of
interest in
job of
matter of
objection to
opportunity for/of
pleasure of/in
point of/in
possibility of
problem of/in
prospect of
purpose of/in
question about/of
reason for
satisfaction of/with
success in
surprise at
task of
thought of
work of
worry about

Noun + infinitive (See page 57.)

ability
agreement
aim
ambition
anxiety
arrangement
attempt
choice
decision
demand
desire
determination
eagerness
failure
intention
need
offer
plan
preparations
promise
proposal
refusal
reluctance
request
time
willingness
wish

Verb + object + infinitive (See page 61.)

advise
allow
announce
ask
assume
authorize
beg
believe
bribe
can't bear
cause
command
compel
consider
dare
declare
discover
drive
enable
encourage
estimate
expect
feel
find
forbid
force
get
hate
help
imagine
instruct
intend
invite
judge
know
lead
leave
like
love
mean (= intend)
mention
need
oblige
order
permit
persuade
prefer
presume
recommend
remind
report
request
require
reveal
show
suppose
take
teach
tell
tempt
train
understand
urge
want
warn
wish

Verb + object + *-ing* form (See page 61.)

avoid
can't help
dislike
dread
enjoy
excuse
hate
imagine
involve
justify
keep
like
love
mean
mind
miss
prevent
remember
resent
risk
save
stop
tolerate
understand